Unlearning God

Unlearning God

How Unbelieving Helped Me Believe

PHILIP GULLEY

Convergent

New York

Library of Congress Cataloging-in-Publication Data
is available upon request.

ISBN 978-1-60142-652-9
Ebook ISBN 978-1-60142-653-6

PRINTED IN THE UNITED STATES OF AMERICA

Book design by Anna Thompson
Jacket design by Jessie Sayward Bright

10 9 8 7 6 5 4 3 2 1

First Edition

To Madeline, my granddaughter,
in hopes she will think deeply,
love widely, and live fearlessly.

And to my mother, Gloria Gulley,
who first taught me how to unlearn,
and died during the writing of this book.

Contents

A Word Before We Start

I began writing this book in my fifty-fifth spring, in my thirty-second year of serving as a Quaker pastor. But the seed of this book began long before that, in my first year of ministry, when I had to decide what kind of pastor I would be. Would I confine myself to the safe boundaries of orthodoxy, or would I question and explore? It occurred to me the people I most admired were spiritual pioneers, pushing themselves, and the church, beyond the settled creeds and doctrines. Besides, I had never been one to follow directions, so it was a foregone conclusion that if there were a straight path to God with clear and printed instructions, I wouldn't take it. Instead, I would wander, meander, and poke along, retain what resonated with my experience, jettison what didn't.

My pattern went something like this. First, I would learn something about God, usually something taught me by the church. I would embrace it as a great truth and believe it with all my heart. Then something would happen—a deep sorrow, a great joy, a revealing discussion, an existential crisis, a painful struggle, an out-of-the-blue insight—that would cause me to reconsider what I'd been taught. Sometimes that was exciting and joyful, other times frightening and upsetting. Sometimes a new insight came quickly, filling the void of the insufficient answer, but most times no new answer rushed in to replace the old. Indeed, there are questions whose answers I will never know.

So first I learned about God, then by virtue of life's events I unlearned, then sometimes I learned again. Because God likes a good joke, I've even recommitted to beliefs I once rejected, like those couples who remarry each other after a decades-long divorce. Sometimes things work better the second time around.

This book is about unlearning things I was taught about God, about myself, about others, about the world. It is about a journey many have taken, so it's not just my story, it could also be told by others. I know that because I'm a pastor and have heard their stories, the fearful confessions of changed minds, the exhilaration of fresh discoveries, the exploration of new territory for which no maps have been drawn.

Sometimes after my unlearning, I have learned something new. If so, I will tell you. Other times I've not found anything new to replace the old, so I can only tell you that the old answer I once held dear no longer suffices. I will even tell you why, but I can't always tell you what belief might replace it. It's a bit like when I was a teenager and my girlfriend broke up with me without having a new boyfriend to take my place. Sometimes life is like that. We know the old isn't working, so we let it go even though we have no idea what might be next.

While writing this book, I was often asked what the title would be. I don't usually reveal book titles before books are published, fearing people won't like them and will tell me so. But I was curious about how people would respond to a book called *Unlearning God,* so this time I answered when asked. A majority of the people were intrigued by the title and pressed me for more details. A few mistakenly assumed I had become an atheist and was writing to convince others to join my ranks.

Many more, when I began to describe the book and its theme, said they had also unlearned certain things about God. A few of them even suggested I write about their experiences and said I could use their names. (People love being mentioned in a book.) Here's where it gets interesting: Some of the people who asked about the book wanted to know if I would tell the readers what to believe. They invariably said the same thing.

"If you're going to tell us what we should no longer believe about God, I hope you tell us what we should believe."

I would say the book wasn't intended to tell them what they should or shouldn't believe. "It is about my experience with God, which might be similar to your experience," I'd say. "As for what to believe, you must figure that out for yourself."

One thing my experience has showed me is that spiritually alive people tend to be insatiably curious about the Divine Presence, refuse to settle for cliché-heavy religion, and feel little obligation to believe something because they are told they must.

I have come to wonder why we've ceded this most intimate of matters to the church and clergy. Yes, thinking deeply about God is challenging work. No doubt about it. But why should someone else do that for us? It would be like paying another person to love our spouses when doing so became too difficult for us. Why are so many people willing to let others do this work for them? Do they believe they're incapable of thinking about God? Are they worried they might think the wrong thing about God and be punished for it? Are they afraid of where doubts and questions might lead? What, or who, made them afraid of thinking for themselves?

Each of the following chapters describes a belief about God I had to unlearn or, at the very least, reinterpret. Each of these beliefs became impossible to sustain, so I chose to let it go, to unlearn it. Now let me drop the bombshell. My unlearning might one day lead me to no longer believe in God, might lead me to give up God altogether. That's the risk. But why should that risk inhibit our search for meaning? Just as every marriage carries the risk of divorce, every relationship of faith carries the risk of unfaith. For me, that hasn't happened yet, although I know and love people for whom it has—people I would have sworn were exempt from existential U-turns. I think no less of them. Indeed, I admire the courage of the thoughtful and sensitive atheist. It is not an easy position to hold in a culture which almost requires a fixed declaration of faith.

Here's another bombshell. The folks I've known who most adamantly believe, who would never confess to a moment of doubt, are often the ones on the verge of unlearning, hoping their doctrinal stubbornness will somehow smother their growing doubts. It doesn't work. I tried. Trust me on this.

The tone of this book is by turns humorous and serious. Sometimes the only fitting response to religious claims is laughter. Nothing pops the balloon of pompous piety more than humor. But seriousness has its place, given the grievous spiritual and emotional harm some beliefs have caused. They must be taken seriously and dismantled thoroughly, as a surgeon might excise a tumor. So sometimes we'll laugh, but most times we'll be thoughtful.

Let's be clear about one thing—unlearning the things we've been taught about God isn't an abandonment of faith. It is in some ways the beginning of faith, the realization that someone else's faith is a poor substitute for our own. But once we decide to be people of faith, we simultaneously commit ourselves to growth and change. We may not realize that at the time, but changes of mind and heart are part and parcel of our spiritual journeys. Avoid those persons who claim always to have believed the same thing and demand you do the same. *What they are really saying is that they have refused to permit their encounters with God to reshape their lives.*

It's always a challenge when writing a book to discern how best to structure it. I didn't have that struggle with this book. It seemed natural to arrange the chapters in a rough chronological order, examining the beliefs in the order I learned them, first in the Catholic Church, then in Quaker meetings, then as I traveled and taught in other denominations. I hasten to add that I've not unlearned everything taught me in those places. Indeed, I've held on to what constitutes the gospel. *God is love.*

I've kept that. *Jesus loved the outsider.* Kept that one, too. *Don't let your religion make you a jerk.* An old Quaker taught me that, and if I were writing a new set of ten commandments, that one would head the list.

Getting back to orthodoxy and exploration. I'm not sure why some folks readily believe everything they're taught and others don't. It would be easy to dismiss the orthodox types as lazy and fearful, and make the exploring types seem brave and thoughtful, but I suspect it's more complex than that. Our spiritual impulses are often deep-seated and not easily surrendered. They are rooted in our personalities, our upbringing, and our life experiences, among other things. They might also be matters of personal preference. Christians who appreciate creeds and doctrines and traditions seem to gravitate toward pastors and churches that value those things. And Christians who value theological exploration tend to seek out churches and pastors who share those passions.

A tragedy of the church is our failure to appreciate the value of both approaches. While I've pitched my tent in the exploration camp, I'm glad there are others who value doctrines, orthodoxy, and tradition. They are the string tethered to the kite creating the tension that makes flight possible. When they become problematic is when they will play out the string only so far, limiting the heights to which we might ascend. While explorer types have often cited the value of theological diversity, many of the orthodox types I've encountered see little value in theological exploration, even though their beliefs, which seem timeless to them, were once the new kids on the block. I can't count the times I've heard "truths" attributed to the apostle

Paul that are clearly products of the American revivalism of the last century. We must disabuse ourselves of the notion that the apostle Paul was a first-century Billy Graham, traveling from city to city preaching a four-point plan of salvation.

If theological and religious exploration doesn't come naturally to you, this book might at first be a bit of a challenge. But you are precisely the people I had in mind when I wrote it. You're like many of the people I've known, loved, and pastored over the years—traditional, conventional, leaning a bit to the right. Even so, you've also questioned and wondered and expressed occasional misgivings about the things you've been taught, if only to yourself. Though it would be difficult to voice your concerns publicly, the questions remain, which might be why you've decided to read a book called *Unlearning God*. I hope it helps. Don't think you must agree with me. That isn't the aim of this book. Read it, engage it, what the heck, write your own book. The best way to articulate what you believe is to put it on paper. Get it out there. Let others chew on it.

After thirty-three years of ministry, I still believe in God, but not the God I believed in decades ago. That God is no more, just like the father I knew as a child isn't the same father. We have a different sort of relationship now. It had to change in order to continue. Thirty-three years ago, I would have said the beliefs I hold now are heretical. Today, I don't use that word, for the moment we dismiss someone else's beliefs while championing our own is the moment our conversation ends and our growth stops. So let the following pages begin our dialogue, a discussion between sincere people seeking a way forward in a world that is vastly different from the world

Jesus inhabited. Invite others to join this conversation. Use it in a Sunday school class. Better yet, gather a few of your friends, invite them to your home, feed them a good meal, and discuss the issues raised in this book. I promise you it will make for a fascinating evening, better than anything on TV.

This life of exploration has meant everything to me. It has kept me connected to a community I love, in a faith tradition I increasingly treasure though still question. I hope this book opens some doors for you. Pack your bags, friend. It's time to explore.

Chapter 1

And So Began
My Life of Doubt

My Baptist father married my Catholic mother in 1955. Ecumenism hadn't been invented yet, so both families were horrified, each certain the other family would roast in hell. Over his parents' objections, my father signed a document promising to raise my siblings and me in the Catholic Church. I was baptized before my father changed his mind; water was sprinkled on me, words were said over me, and I was saved, just like that, a member of the One True Church, destined for heaven, along with my family, except my father, which is why I cried when the priest sprinkled me with water, sensing even then my dad was screwed.

The nuns urged me to pray for my father, in the hope he would see the error of his way, dispense with heresy, and embrace the true faith of St. Peter, the first pope and Jesus's best friend. I ran the idea past my father, who seemed curiously uninterested in joining the One True Church. Since there was only so much I could do, I handed the problem over to God and let him worry about it.*

The One True Church swarmed with children, roomfuls of kids of all ages. Families with eight, nine, and ten kids. Families so large the parents stopped naming their children and assigned them numbers. Church services were held every morning, and twice on Saturdays and Sundays, to accommodate everyone. A dozen people would cram in a pew that comfortably seated six. Kids stacked two and three deep. In terms of sheer numbers, we beat every church in town. Two nuns ran the show. Fifty kids jammed in a room learning the Catechism, the nuns circling us, rendering us mute with fear.

This was back in the days when nuns wore habits, before they got sneaky and went undercover, dressing like the rest of us to blend in and catch us sinning. It now seems ironic that the priests and nuns populating my childhood wore black and white. I'm not sure which ancient cleric picked the colors, but I wonder now if it were intentional, even sacramental, an outward sign of an inward reality. Black and white. True and false. Good and evil. Heaven and hell. In or out. No in between. No shades of gray. No dash of color. No nuance. No straying from the reservation. So my father was out, as were the billions of people not fortunate enough to be Catholic.

It wasn't just the Catholics with the lock on heaven. The

---

* When I was a kid, God was a him. By the time I went to college and seminary to study theology, God was a him and a her. Someday we'll create a pronoun just for God that will please everyone.

Protestants were also sending one another to hell in record numbers. I would later become a Quaker, one of the most peaceable denominations in the history of Christianity, and even some of them cheerfully sentenced certain people to hell. But when one's own father is condemned to hell, it's hard to think well of the institution sending him there. Not only hard to think well of the institution but hard to take it seriously when it spoke about God and Jesus and love. I wanted to believe in Jesus, in God, in the One True Church, but the One True Church made that nearly impossible.

I was eight years old, maybe nine, and a nun, I can't remember her name, told me if I hated God, I would die.

"How soon?" I asked.

I was a stickler for details.

"God will strike you down that very moment," she said.

So that night I put her to the test, under my blankets, whispering, "I hate God, I hate God, I hate God." Three times, one for each person of the Trinity.

I whispered because I shared a bedroom with my brother David and didn't want him to hear me and tell our parents, who would most certainly have done something, even if God didn't. Besides, if God knew our every thought, as I had been taught, then God could certainly hear my whispers. Or not, because I wasn't struck down that very moment, which left me to conclude that either God didn't strike down people who hated him or God couldn't know our every thought, which meant the nun was full of beans.

And so began my life of doubt.

My words seem evil now, when I see them in black and

white, like something the bratty girl in *The Exorcist* might say, and I'm surprised my head didn't spin 360 degrees and I didn't vomit green goop. Instead, I went to sleep and woke up the next morning blessedly alive.

Maybe God knew I didn't mean it, that I was testing the nun, so in a moment of grace, as is God's habit, elected not to smite me. And I didn't mean it. Given my inexperience, I neither loved nor hated God. Mostly, God mystified me. Did he live up in the clouds or inside me? Did I disgust him or please him? Did God love everyone, or love some and hate others? Was God a capitalist or a communist? A Republican or a Democrat? A Catholic or a Protestant? A him or a her? And the biggest question of all—did God even exist?

Yes, God existed, my parents said, and was a Republican, my father assured me. And a Catholic, my mother said. And a male, our priest, Father McLaughlin, said. Though I no longer trusted the nun, I was hoping God was a Catholic and looking down from heaven every Sunday morning to see me kneeling at St. Mary's Queen of Peace Catholic Church and thinking well of me. I had since confessed to hating God to our priest, who took it in stride, and told me to say three Hail Marys and two Our Fathers and I would be forgiven, which I did, to be on the safe side.

The safe side defined my early spirituality. After testing God once and surviving the encounter, I decided not to push my luck, so I went through first communion and became an altar boy, waking up early on Saturday mornings to serve the Mass, hoping God noticed that, too. It was an era of détente. I no longer tested God, and in exchange, God didn't strike me dead. If Richard Nixon could strike a deal with China, I figured I could strike one with God.

God apparently loved deals. If I belonged to the One True Church and went to Mass every Sunday, I'd go to heaven when I died. Or so the nuns told me. Then after the deal was inked, I read the fine print. No eating meat on Fridays, no skipping confession on Saturday night, no attending the Baptist church with my sister, who had jumped the Catholic ship, hooked up with the Baptists, and was headed straight to hell. The nun had mentioned none of this when I joined. I had been hoodwinked, taken for a ride, falling for the oldest trick in the book, one hand moving the walnut shells, the other hand hiding the pea.

"What if I ever leave the One True Church?" I asked the nun.

"When you die, you will spend eternity apart from God, in eternal torment," she said.

"How do you know?"

"Because I'm a nun," she said.

Then she warned Father McLaughlin I bore watching and he caught me alone in the altar boy room and told me I had disappointed God.

"How do you know?" I asked.

"Because I'm a priest," he said.

This was back in the days when religious authorities were widely admired and generally believed, so I prayed every Sunday for God to forgive me and vowed to walk the straight and narrow and become a priest when I was older so I, too, could scare small children and get them right with God. I told no one except Father McLaughlin, one Sunday morning while preparing for Mass, who seemed elated with the notion but failed to mention I wouldn't be able to marry and would have to sit alone in my house each night trying not to think of girls, which I was just then starting to do.

I decided to talk it over with the nun.

"What happens if I become a priest, then fall in love and leave the Church to get married?"

"When you die, you will spend eternity apart from God, in eternal torment," she said.

The Church was nothing if not consistent.

But I wondered how they knew these things. How could they speak with such certainty? Certainty seemed the highest value of every religious person I knew. Their church had the Truth, capital *T,* and no one else. Joe, my best friend in the fourth grade, was a Jehovah's Witness and just as certain his church was the One True Church. He gave me pamphlets to read at recess, urging me toward Jehovah, who apparently was opposed to birthdays, Christmas, and Halloween, which I took as a sign I shouldn't join.

But what if the Jehovah's Witnesses were right, and the Catholic Church was wrong? What if the Baptists were right? Or the half dozen folks who had started up a new church, meeting every Sunday morning in a dinky house on the main street in our town? What if out of all the churches in the world, those half dozen people had nailed it on the head and were the One True Church, the culmination of God's great plan to save the world? I went to school with one of them, so buddied up to her on the off chance the world ended and I could ride her coattails into heaven. Then the next year the pastor went crazy, the church disbanded, and a lawyer bought the house and set out his shingle.

To the best of my knowledge, there were no lawyers at St. Mary's Queen of Peace, the lawyers in our town having money and the Catholics tending not to. We were the church of labor. One did not join the Catholic Church to get ahead in the community. We had ceded that territory to the Methodists and Episcopalians, both of whom worshipped in new buildings. We met in a flat-roofed building on Main Street next to Pleas Lilly's Citgo gas station. It appeared we had run out of money while building the church so stopped after one story. It wasn't the kind of structure to inspire meditation and high thoughts. The windows were painted shut, it didn't have air-conditioning, and in the summertime we dropped like flies, fainting from the heat, our heads thumping the pews like watermelons.

What we Catholics did have going for us was longevity, which we believed to be an indication of God's favor. We were the first church, instituted by Jesus, the Bride of Christ, launched by St. Peter, the first pope. What we lacked in building, we made up for in pedigree. The Episcopalians, the Methodists, the Jehovah's Witnesses, the half dozen people who met on Sundays in the dinky house, were newcomers, pretenders to the throne. We believed our institutional durability was an indication not of skilled management, historical accident, or strategic political alliances but of God's seal of approval.

I didn't wonder about it then, but I wonder now why it is that God's favor seems always to be indicated by the one quality we possess in spades. Let a church endure, and it must surely be an indication of its chosenness. Let a church be large and wealthy, and it must surely be an indication of God's favor. Let a church be small and poor, and it must be surely be an indication of God's preference for the underdog.

Why this tendency to single out our one defining trait and claim it as proof of God's favor?

While we're thinking about that, let's think also about the spiritual implications of our claims to divine favor. The moment we believe God is uniquely for us, we simultaneously imply God isn't for others. The moment we claim to be the One True Church, we claim the other churches are not true, that their encounters with God, and their collective life with Jesus, is less than ours.

Joe and I would argue about this on the playground, staking out our territory. I, a member of the One True Church; he, a member of Jehovah's true community, each of us lowering himself to be with the other. By then, I was serving as an altar boy several times a week and was Father McLaughlin's go-to guy. Joe was basking in the glow of his recent baptism, working the playground for converts, aiming to be one of Jehovah's 144,000 elect. Though we were friends, it eventually became clear one of us would have to throw in the towel and join the other. When that didn't happen, we drifted apart.

Our separation was the nearly inevitable consequence of the exclusive beliefs we had been taught. In our efforts to draw near to God, we learned to mistrust others. When my Baptist father married my Catholic mother, his uncle wrote to warn him the pope would take their children. He urged my father not to proceed with the wedding, that it wouldn't last. We had a good laugh over that at my parents' fiftieth anniversary dinner.

I once went to visit an elderly member of my Quaker meeting. He hadn't been active in our meeting since my arrival as its pastor, but I had visited him several times and had enjoyed our time together. Though I introduced myself, he mistook me for someone else. He was nearly deaf and could barely see. I was able, after much shouting, to make him understand I brought greetings from our Quaker meeting.

"Did you hear what they've gone and done?" he asked.

"What who has gone and done?" I asked.

"Our Quaker meeting. They've gone and hired a Catholic."

I realized he was referring to me.

"The Catholics sent him to turn us into a Catholic church," he said.

I didn't correct the man. He was well past ninety-five and starting to experience dementia. And he had been kind to me in the past, so I simply changed the subject and enjoyed our time together. But on the way home, I imagined the pope, surrounded by his cardinals, pointing to a map of central Indiana, saying, "I want that little Quaker meeting. Is Gulley still with us? Send him."

Yes, I was a sleeper agent for the Catholic Church, worming my way into the Religious Society of Friends at the age of sixteen, slowly gaining their trust until I was encouraged to become a pastor, then enrolling in college and graduate school, becoming recorded as a Quaker minister, pastoring one Quaker meeting after another, building my credentials, until I would be invited to pastor a meeting outside Indianapolis in order to lead its 120 souls into the waiting bosom of the Roman Catholic Church.*

On the day I was recorded as a Quaker minister, I invited my Catholic grandparents to come watch. Afterward, my grandmother hugged me, tearful, then told me I was the first one in our family in over six hundred years to leave the Catholic Church. Someone snapped a picture of us. It was my grandmother's first time in a Protestant church, and she looked terrified, clutching her handbag to her bosom, fearful God would find her there and strike her dead.

But isn't this what must be moved beyond—the gripping fear that God's family is so small, God's love so narrow, it has no room for others? I understand the appeal of exclusivity, of believing God is uniquely for us. I bet you do, too. It's flattering when others make the same choices we've made. It serves to confirm our wisdom and validate our decisions. But when we do that with religion, we create insiders and outsiders, and before long the outsider is not only wrong, he is our enemy, the one against whom we must prevail.

When I was a kid, a neighbor told me there was only one way to mow a lawn, in stripes perpendicular to the street. After decades of his mowing in the same pattern, his lawn was a series of parallel ruts. It served as a visual reminder that one-way thinking leaves us in a rut. Similarly, single-minded faith leaves us entrenched and stuck. And so for me, there can

---

* Quaker ministers aren't ordained, since ordination implies the church has the power to grant (or ordain) the gifts of ministry. Instead, we record, or acknowledge, that God has already given someone the gifts for ministry and in recording or acknowledging those gifts, we invite the person to use them.

be no One True Church. There are only people who have, by accidents of time, birth, geography, and ancestry, approached God differently. Consider my story. I was born into a Catholic family in a small midwestern town. By then, the Catholics had been around only 1,900 years, though anthropologists believe humans have possessed the ability to think symbolically, a necessary element of religious practice, for about 100,000 years. The particular Catholic church I attended had existed less than forty years when I was born. Prior to that, the nearest Catholic church was several towns away, so my mother, had we moved to town a generation earlier, might well have decided to attend the Methodist church on the next block, or the Quaker meeting down the street, or the Baptist church five blocks away. Given the many twists and turns my life might have taken, how is it possible God orchestrated events to my benefit? There were tens of millions of people born in 1961, so why me, and not others?

Of course, one could look at the matter differently. One could believe truth isn't measured by longevity, or status, or obedience to Scripture. One could believe true religion is practiced wherever mercy, peace, and justice flower. One could believe true religion isn't a matter of correct categories but a matter of compassion. One could believe the exclusivity of the One True Church or the Only Way to God is a gross denial of God's wide participation in the human story. One could reject altogether our selfish insistence that we alone hold the monopoly on truth and faith.

The nuns and priests of my childhood were like all of us— they were teaching what they were taught. Perhaps as they grew older, they changed their minds. After all, I did. Now I believe there is no One True Church, no One True Faith, no single path to God. There are only compassion and grace, and where they are found, God is present, yearning to know and be known. This God transcends our human barriers, loving and living far beyond the tidy categories we've created. This God understands our human need to feel special but doesn't want that need to come at the expense of others, so in that mysterious, ironic way of the Divine, can love us uniquely, while loving others distinctively, too. Just as I love my two sons differently, and yet the same.

God's love is a gift to celebrate, not a status to covet. We are on the way to understanding life when we realize God's love for others in no way diminishes God's love for us. This love is not predicated upon our church affiliation, our religion, or our spiritual status. It is not confined to the innocent of heart or the doctrinally pure. While it is true that spiritual maturity helps us appreciate God's love more deeply, it does not increase God's love for us, which is already infinite. The great truth is this—whether we are Catholic, Baptist, Methodist, or Quaker; whether we are Hindu, Buddhist, Muslim, or Jewish; whether we believe with all our hearts or don't believe at all, we are members, all of us, of the true community of God.

Why It Matters

The expansive nature of God's love is the foundation of each principle I will discuss in this book. I place little value on doctrine, except the rule of love. Nor do I worship at the altar of tradition, unless that tradition helps us love. I do not even value the Bible, unless it empowers us to love others more fully. Absent love, it is no more sacred than a telephone book. Love was God's first gesture, indeed, is God's only gesture. True life begins not at conception, and not even at birth, but when we love. Love is our pulse.

Our lifelong movement toward love gives shape and meaning to our lives. All other aspirations, be they financial, vocational, or relational, will never satisfy if love is absent. We are only now comprehending the role of DNA in our formation, though we often ignore the power of love in shaping our lives. I know parents who spare no expense when it comes to their children's education and status, believing their children's success and happiness in life hinge on material wealth, but do little to cultivate love, as if it were incidental to human joy.

Likewise, some churches seem so enthralled with orthodoxy they have forgotten to love, despite our longing for communities enlivened by grace. I was speaking with a pastor once whose passion for right belief was so strong he alienated nearly everyone he met. Every place and every person he touched withered. When I asked him the role of love in the gospel, he said it was beside the point. Not satisfied with purifying his own church, he wanted to cleanse his denomination, so finagled his way onto a board of oversight where he managed to divide a religious organization that had not seen a split in over a hundred years. Our failure to love, our insistence on our own privilege at the expense of others, causes many of our divisions. It tears asunder churches, families, businesses, civic organizations, societies, and governments.

Can we make love, not exclusion, our spiritual foundation, lest our lives and spirits wither and die?

Chapter 2

We Revered Women Too Much
to Let Them Lead

I met my first nun at the peak of their popularity, when the highest honor a Catholic girl could conceive of was joining a convent and not conceiving, an aspiration aided by the burka-like habit she was made to wear.* Despite this obvious drawback, 7,000 women a year were joining the Catholic orders in the early sixties. In 1965, when I was four years old, there were 180,000 nuns in America, most of them named for men, given the Catholic Church's aversion to all things female, except for Mary, whom they idolized because of her rare ability to bear children without ever having sex. So deep was the Catholics' admiration for Mary, they named every female some

---

* You can gauge the rights of women in any religious tradition by the clothing they're required to wear. Generally speaking, the more clothes, the less freedom. How about we just tell the women to dress comfortably and tell the men to exercise self-control?

variation of her name—Mary, Marie, Marian, Maria, Marilee, Marilyn, Maribelle, Marybeth, and Maryann. Before the age of ten, I had met three nuns named Mary John, one Mary Paul, and a Peter Marie. It seemed perfectly normal then, but now I wonder why any woman would have stayed in a church that held such a low regard for her gender that its women had to be named for men.

My mother taught at a Catholic school, so nuns were a staple of my childhood—nuns at the dinner table, nuns at weekend cookouts, nuns on vacation, nuns as babysitters. I couldn't swing a dead penguin without hitting a nun. One of the nuns, a regular visitor to our home, turned in her robe, left the convent, and moved to an apartment in the city. I was young when it happened and amazed that such a thing was even permitted. My little brother, David, asked me what would become of her.

"When she dies, she will spend eternity apart from God, in eternal torment," I said.

Despite my proximity to nuns, they frightened me. They reminded me of God, who I had the impression didn't like kids, since he and Mary had only one child and that hadn't gone well. God especially didn't like it when kids laughed in church, even when old Mr. Muller, seated in the pew in front of us, passed gas, an exclamation point tacked on to the responsorial psalm. How could God not find that hysterical? I bowed my head and bit the inside of my mouth, squeezing my eyes shut, struggling not to laugh, until the nun sitting behind me, Sister Peter Marie, pulled my ear, hard, and hissed at me not to laugh in church, that it was a sin.

I was keeping a list of sins and committing it to memory, lest I inadvertently commit one and spend eternity apart from

God in eternal torment. I went home and added *Laughing in Church* to the list, right after *Kissing* and just before *Murder.* By the age of seven, I had kissed only one girl, Bridgett Howard, who was six years old and Catholic and should have known better. Our families were friends, and during a visit to their home she lured me behind her father's La-Z-Boy and smooched me smack on the lips, which I reported to Father McLaughlin the next Saturday at confession, and was fined three Hail Marys and two Our Fathers, even though it hadn't been my idea. Still, it could have been worse. I could have murdered someone, in which case I would have had to say four Hail Marys and three Our Fathers.

Nuns, I was fairly certain, never kissed anyone, so I was a bit suspicious when they told me it was a sin, suspecting they were criminalizing the one behavior they weren't tempted to commit. None of the nuns I knew were at risk of being kissed, either. They were all old as fungus, St. Mary's Queen of Peace being the last stop before death. There was no way out. We were the Fargo of the Roman Catholic Church, the place where hope died. A nun had only to step off the bus in front of Pleas Lilly's gas station and glimpse the church to realize she had royally honked someone off or that her end was near.

Of the nuns populating my childhood, two were especially prominent—Sister Therese and Sister Rosalie. Sister Therese grew weary of the church and the men who ran it, so gave up the nunhood. For a nun, she was my kind of gal, witty and cynical, two of the virtues I admire most in a woman. Sister Rosalie was round and jolly and visited our home frequently, baking us cookies, cakes, and pies, then knocking back a cold one with my father on our front porch, an all-purpose nun.

What confuses me now, as I look back, was the nuns' willingness to cooperate with their captivity. These were strong and thoughtful women, more than capable of leading the church, probably more so than the priests I knew, who tended to be one-dimensional, knowing all sorts of things about weird church stuff but next to nothing about practical matters, since everything was done for them, mostly by nuns. I wondered why the nuns didn't go on strike—no more teaching, no more cooking for the priest, no more cleaning the church, no more spinning the roulette wheel at Monte Carlo Night to raise money for the parish. No more nothing, until the church came to its senses and admitted women to the ranks of leadership.

When I was older, I asked a priest why women weren't permitted to serve in the highest levels of church administration. He said, "We revere women too much to let them lead." In their world, women could change diapers, clean toilets, and wipe butts but were otherwise so dainty their hands couldn't be soiled by the grime of governance.

Regrettably, the sexism of my childhood wasn't confined to Catholicism, or to my childhood, for that matter. It still infects nearly every denomination in Christianity, sometimes with the hearty cooperation of the women, who, even as the boot of oppression is pressed against their necks, believe it is God's will. I once attended a Quaker meeting that was searching for a new pastor and heard several women voice their objection to hiring a woman. "A pastor ought to be a man," they said. Women have their hands full dealing with the patriarchs of the church, they shouldn't have to battle the matriarchs, too.

We've now had a U.S. presidential election featuring a female candidate nominated by a major political party. Had Hillary Clinton been elected America's commander in chief and chief executive, she would have overseen nearly 2.5 million military personnel, supervised almost 3 million federal employees, administered an annual budget of nearly $4 trillion, negotiated treaties on behalf of the United States, and would have still been told that by virtue of her gender she was incapable of leading a fundamental Baptist church of thirty-five people in Bugtussle, Kentucky, or a Roman Catholic church anywhere in the world, or a Mormon church, or a Jehovah's Witnesses congregation, or a Southern Baptist church, or a Missouri Synod Lutheran congregation, or some Quaker meetings, or many Jewish synagogues and Muslim mosques, all because she lacked a male appendage, the one characteristic apparently necessary for spiritual leadership. Ironically, that same appendage has gotten countless male leaders in hot water, so I'm not questioning its power, just its necessity for leadership.

I once was present at an interfaith dialogue attended by a number of Mormons. During the question-and-answer session, a woman, not of the Mormon faith, asked a Mormon woman present what it was like being excluded from every significant position of leadership in her church. The questioner asked it kindly, sincerely wanting to know how she felt as a woman in a male-dominated church. The Mormon woman's face went blank, and she said, almost robotically, as if she stood in front of a mirror every morning saying it over and over, "I feel fulfilled as a woman in the Mormon church."

Her husband was seated beside her, and when the question was asked, he placed his arm around her shoulders, as if physically keeping her in her place. I remember to this day her blank expression and the mechanical tone in her voice, repeating from memory a statement learned long before.

Think of the energy those churches must expend to convince women they aren't suited for leadership. Why so many women continue to believe their inferior status is God's plan mystifies me. This poisonous mind-set has relegated women to the backseats of the church's bus; has viewed women as perpetual Eves leading Adam astray; has kept women silent, submissive, and enslaved; and would die overnight of its own tired weight if women no longer cooperated with their own bondage, and if men of goodwill demanded its end.

It is, of course, incredibly difficult to overcome centuries of sexism, especially when that sexism is rooted in the "sacred" teachings of a faith. Those who exclude women cite Paul's admonition in 1 Corinthians 14 requiring women to remain silent in church, or Paul's first letter to Timothy forbidding a woman to teach or exercise authority over a man. Since Christians who hold these views are often literalists, it does no good to point out that many reputable scholars doubt these verses originated with Paul. What matters to these Christians isn't authorship, after all, but the mere fact of these verses' presence in their infallible Bible. And what if we knew for a fact Paul did believe such things? Paul also believed illnesses were caused by demonic spirits, but outside of Appalachia and a few zip codes in Mississippi, it's a rare church nowadays that requires our assent to that.

Think of the hypocrisy of a church that forbids women from

leadership while depending upon them to survive. Attend any church, anywhere in the world, and you'll notice a preponderance of women giving generously of their time, passion, and resources to keep their churches afloat, often while their pastors denigrate their gender with stories and sermons that stereotype and diminish them. Once, while attending a Christian book convention at which thousands of women were present, I heard an evangelist describe women as flighty, overemotional, dim-witted, materialistic, and shallow, to the amusement and agreement of many of the men present. I thought of the many bright women I know, stood, and left. Why the women in that place didn't also rise to their feet and walk out baffled me. Were we to lift out the word *woman* and substitute *African-American* or *Jewish* or *Hispanic,* we would be rightly appalled, but many Christians have become so accustomed to misogyny, we scarcely blink.

The absence of women in leadership has created a church in which the worst attributes of men have grown unchecked— the manipulation of process to gain personal power, the abuse of children, the unrelenting patriarchy that values rank and privilege at the expense of equality and justice, not to mention the rampant sexual harassment of women that has only recently come to light. When the moderating influence of women is excluded, religious institutions become unbalanced and unhealthy. Just as any church that failed to cultivate the masculine perspective would be out of balance, so has the church's historic marginalization of women harmed its well-being. One has only to look at the scandals of abuse plaguing the church and culture to see firsthand the staggering cost of male privilege.

I serve a Quaker meeting that for thirteen years called two persons to pastoral leadership, my copastor, Jennifer, and me. Jennifer's ability to "read" situations and people, her well-honed instinct, was uncanny. She often addressed challenges before I even perceived an issue existed. Her gifts for leadership were part and parcel of the female experience. She felt, thought, and led in a way I couldn't, in a manner informed by her motherhood, by her nurturing qualities, by her intelligence, by her spiritual maturity. She was an excellent pastor because she was a woman, not in spite of it.*

But even if Jennifer hadn't been a mother, she would still have brought to the role a perspective I couldn't bring. Her experience of being a woman in America, of being shunted to the side, of living in a country that lacks the political will to enshrine in its Constitution the innate equality of women, that very experience informed her ministry in a way my life of privilege never could. Having fought every day for rights and liberties I take for granted, she was quicker to see systemic injustice and aggression where I have been blinded by the status quo.

I understand the desire of male-centered people of faith to please God. I understand their fear at angering a deity they believe has the power to punish them for eternity. If I believed in the God they believe in, I'd be afraid, too. While I don't share their understanding of God, my disagreement doesn't

---

* I'm speaking of her in the past tense not because she died but because she retired from pastoral ministry. Not a day passes that I don't miss her considerable gifts.

allay their fears, which are real to them. But I would say this to them: In the long history of Christianity we have embraced institutional and theological changes many times. The early Christians believed they could remain a part of the Hebrew faith of Israel. Over time, it became clear they couldn't, so they began moving away from their spiritual heritage to create a new religion. (Unfortunately, we didn't leave behind the anti-Semitism which arose in our early days.) For centuries, Christians believed slavery was ordained by God, and quoted the Bible to defend their views, though in time the church left behind that understanding.* Today, many Christians have rejected the Bible's condemnation of homosexuality in order to embrace what they believe to be the greater biblical imperative of love and compassion. I know some Christians haven't yet made that shift, but odds are their children or grandchildren will, making their intransigence seem all the more irrational.

So it is with the church's resistance to women in leadership, which is crippling it just when the world needs a thoughtful, inclusive, and creative Christianity. We face global crises of income inequality, religious radicalism, environmental calamity, and military adventurism, all of which threaten our well-being. The church can play a vital role in solving these problems, but not if we are hindered by the outdated rejection of some of our most capable people. We have entered the battle for moral and ethical progress with one hand tied behind our backs.

To elevate men at the expense of women is to repudiate a

---

* Or became more subtle in their racism. Take your pick.

woman's God-given worth and should therefore be rejected by everyone who claims to love and follow God. The rejection of women from leadership is not only a disservice to humanity but an insult to God. How can the denigration and denial of women's potential be pleasing to the God who created them, the God who has gifted them with incredible gifts, only to have the church scorn those gifts in order to perpetuate male power and privilege? Any religion whose members can't stand equally before God and one another is a flawed religion, deserving neither our deference nor our devotion.

The first twenty-six years of my life, I attended churches led by male pastors, then began copastoring a Quaker meeting, sharing leadership responsibility with a woman. I would later learn that the reason I had been hired was that that Quaker meeting, located in a rural part of the state, had come under fire from other Christians in the area for employing a female pastor. Rather than defend their female pastor, they hired me, so they could say to their neighbors, "We have a man as our pastor, too." I learned this only after they had fired me for not believing in hell. I apologized to the woman, telling her I would never have agreed to serve as their copastor had I known the real reason for my employment. She responded graciously, assuring me she had appreciated the extra help I had provided, even though my tenure was brief. Despite that congregation's unwillingness to stand by their pastor, she remained several years, all the while knowing the people she ministered to so faithfully had such little regard for her gender they couldn't summon the courage to tell busybodies and bullies to mind their own business. Every woman in ministry I have ever met can tell a similar story—the failure of a congregation to appreciate the leadership of a woman, which if offered by a man would be gratefully received.

Of course, religion is not the only field in which women are underappreciated. This unfortunate trend is nearly universal. I've seen gifted females denied a pastoral role because of their gender, only to see hired a much less capable male pastor, who proceeded to wreck the church with his incompetence. Today, the Roman Catholic Church faces a shortage of priests, a shortage which would disappear overnight if that institution were to shed its resistance to female leadership. Perhaps the decline of the Southern Baptist denomination could be reversed if their leadership included women, for what young and thoughtful woman today can joyfully participate in a faith that excludes her from full participation in its community?

I don't believe the church is divinely protected from the consequences of its folly. In Matthew 16:18, Jesus said about Peter, "Upon this rock I will build my church; and the gates of Hades will not overpower it." While I can't help but wonder if some early church bureaucrats snuck that in to legitimize their movement, it's not Hades we have to fear. If the church can't offer a full and hearty welcome to all its people, our death will be self-inflicted. And who knows, with an obstructive church out of the way, God might start up a fresh faith, one that values the heart over certain other organs.

Why It Matters

For the first half of my life, I worshipped a God I believed called only men to church leadership. This is what I had been taught, and I accepted it without question. While I was not hateful toward women, I was perfectly comfortable excluding them from pastoral ministry and felt no obligation to advocate for their inclusion. My heart and mind were changed when listening to a sermon given on the eleventh chapter of Acts, when Peter dreamed of a sheet lowered from heaven containing animals forbidden in the Torah to eat. Ordered three times to prepare the animals and eat them, Peter refused, claiming they were unfit. Each time, a voice responded, "What God has made clean, you must not profane." I was in my late teens, visiting a friend's church. The pastor giving the sermon was not preaching about women in leadership, but it struck me in an instant that God had gifted men and women alike with gifts for ministry, and that my denial of those gifts was a denial of God.

That day was an important unlearning for me. Since that moment, I have unlearned other "truths" I once believed. At each crossway, my vision of God has grown, just as your understanding of God has increased as you've traveled truth's road. Now I believe God equips us all to teach what we've been taught, granting each of us the joy and responsibility of sharing all that is holy, all that is right, all that is good.

As I unlearned God's preference for males, I also had to unlearn other biases I once cultivated. I began to see the presence of God in people of color, not having realized before the extent to which my childhood culture had diminished their value. I learned to love and appreciate gay people, and see beyond their sexuality. Years later, when a leader in our denomination demanded my obedience to a small-minded policy I found hateful, I refused, knowing my rejection of one group would lead inevitably to the rejection of others.

Have you noticed the domino effect present in all our prejudices? We are seldom satisfied to despise just one group but tend to keep looking for more "others" and "lesser thans" to oppress and exclude. Whenever we hate one, we will inevitably continue hating until we loathe even ourselves.

As I reflect on this matter now, I believe I learned exclusion early on because it was so ingrained in the church's teachings. Even when they weren't blatantly stated, the church's biases were quite obvious, and still widely accepted as God's preferred pattern for humanity. These patterns aren't easily shed, so they continue to haunt and harm our faith communities. What we must begin to imagine is a church that has outgrown its biases, a church faithful to God's wide and holy vision.

Chapter 3

———

My Unbroken Chain
of Impure Thoughts

Sometimes when people find out I'm a pastor, they make it a point to tell me they don't go to church, even though I didn't ask. It's an odd thing about being a minister and might be unique to our vocation. I've never heard anyone tell a salesperson they don't buy things, or mention to a firefighter they don't believe in fire, or tell a pilot or bus driver they avoid transportation.

I understand why people don't go to church. When I was a kid, I didn't want to go, and I wouldn't have, except that Father McLaughlin told me if I didn't, I'd go to hell. He didn't single me out personally, he didn't point his finger at me and say, "Gulley, if you don't go to church, you'll die and go to hell." His warnings were general in nature, delivered during sermons to a church full of people, but it didn't take a rocket scientist to know we had one foot in hell and the other on a banana peel.

Were it not for the nuns, Father McLaughlin, Bishop

Biskup, and the pope interceding on our behalf, we would have been goners. I had never even met Bishop Biskup, despite praying for him every week as instructed. But I imagined any man strong enough to beat back the devil and keep me from hell had to be quite a physical specimen, so I was surprised when Bishop Biskup visited St. Mary's and turned out to be small and mousy, sporting a bad comb-over and thick glasses. I was pretty certain Ol' Scratch could take him. Fortunately, the nuns were robust, and I had every confidence they could protect me if push came to shove.

Though I was having my doubts about religion, I went to church every Sunday morning and confession every Saturday night, the forgiveness of sins being an essential component of the pure in heart, which I wasn't, but tried to be, and would have been if it weren't for my brothers, who led me into temptation every chance they could. If it hadn't been for Father McLaughlin putting in a good word for me, I would have been sunk. I imagined him pleading with God, pointing out my nobler traits, which I made sure he learned about at confession.

"Forgive me, Father, for I have sinned. It has been one week since my last confession. I said a bad word this week when I was mowing Mrs. Harvey's yard for free. And I had an impure thought when I was rescuing Karen Conners from drowning in the pool."

My adolescence was an unbroken chain of impure thoughts, which I dutifully confessed to Father McLaughlin each Saturday, clearing the slate, to make room for a whole new batch of impure thoughts in the week ahead. The point of confession, I was taught, was to prepare me for receiving holy communion the next morning at Mass. Father McLaughlin would raise up a piece of bread and a cup of wine, and they would become Christ's actual body and blood, the Catholics believed, though they still tasted like bread and wine to me.

"How is this possible?" I asked Father McLaughlin. "How do bread and wine become body and blood?"

"It surpasses understanding," he said.

It certainly did.

I would later study theology at a Catholic university and learn it was called *transubstantiation,* which in Latin means "something we don't understand, but sounds impressive when done by a priest." It worked. I was very impressed. I tried transubstantiation at home, with Wonder bread and Welch's grape juice, but nothing happened. It did feel different at church, with Father McLaughlin, the bread melting on my tongue, the bitter tang of the wine, which they gave me to drink even though I wasn't of drinking age.

Catholicism was one delicious mystery after another—the incense, the holy water we dabbed on our foreheads entering and leaving the sanctuary, the stations of the cross, where the death of Jesus played out on plaques hung on the wall so even the illiterate could know the story, or so I eventually learned. Central to this great mystery was the power of the priest to announce the pardon of our sins, which I found most comforting, given my proclivities. I envied the priests their power, and for a good part of my childhood I thought of becoming a priest so I could dangle the carrot of heaven before my enemy, just out of reach. I had only one enemy, who wasn't even Catholic, so I wasn't sure my being a priest would pose a threat to him, but I was willing to try.

Technically, of course, I knew we all had the power to forgive, but those who crossed me seemed curiously uninterested in my forgiveness and kept right on annoying me. It wasn't the power of forgiveness I was interested in so much as the power to not forgive if the mood struck me, to stand between God and another, able to open the flow of blessing or shut it off, like the wizard in Oz behind the curtain, working the levers. This kind of power is so intoxicating, it's no wonder the Catholic Church claimed it for themselves. Then again, this might be a marketing strategy found in all religions: to create a perceived need, in this case for forgiveness, then rather conveniently be the only ones to fill it.

I wish Quakers were exempt from such plotting and power grabs, but we could give the Roman Curia a run for its money, proving that manipulative religion is not only widespread but also intractable, something we seem unable or unwilling to shed. This lust for power has always plagued the church, indeed, plagued nearly every culture. Even before Jesus was dead, his followers were contending for power—bickering about who would rule in heaven, who would have God's ear and be God's intermediary, the mediator between God and humanity.

So I went to confession, because I was taught that the priest, and only the priest, had the power to confer God's forgiveness. At the time, I didn't find it suspicious that the folks telling me that were priests. I simply accepted it as the truth, as an inviolate rule of the universe. I believed it as I believed in gravity or oxygen or the honesty of Richard Nixon. (I was seriously confused as a child.)

When I was a teenager a friend invited me to attend his Quaker meeting, where I discovered that the belief in a priest's intercessory powers was confined largely to the Catholic and Orthodox churches. Indeed, the fervor with which the Quakers rejected priestly intercession was startling. They told me, before I even asked, that I could speak to God directly, and that God would speak back, especially if I sat quietly and listened, which further alarmed me, since sitting quietly generally led to impure thoughts. Still, it was good to know I could ask God directly to forgive my impure thoughts.

Looking back, I realize it wasn't the idea of confession I found unsettling. I even found the experience cathartic, though it was a little embarrassing to disclose the darker side of my personality to a priest who didn't seem to be paying attention. He never engaged me in further conversation and almost always dispensed the same penalty. I might as well have been talking to a machine. Of course, listening to hundreds of people confess the same midwestern sins week after week had to be excruciating. On television, people in New York City entered the confessional and confessed to murder, but at St. Mary's our confessions were more innocuous. *Forgive me, Father, for I have sinned. I have failed to be all that God wants me to be.* We knew what people were confessing, because Father McLaughlin was deaf as a post and we had to shout our sins. Once a year or so someone would confess something specific and salacious—a torrid affair, a theft, eating meat on Friday—and we would have to shun that person for the rest of his life in order to protect our church from contamination. God forgave him, since that was God's job, but we were a different matter.

What I found most troubling, as I look back, was the church's insertion of the middleman, the notion we couldn't stand on our own two legs, look God in the eye, metaphorically speaking, and be friends. In time, I realized almost every church denied our ability to do just that. If it weren't the Catholics and Orthodox insisting on the necessity of a priest, it was evangelicals insisting on the necessity of Jesus interceding for us. Though Jesus modeled spiritual intimacy with God, he apparently didn't mean to imply we could enjoy the same sort of relationship. Of course, the Jesus who mediated for us was always the Jesus whose values and priorities were curiously similar to our own.

We need a middleman, they said, because we lack the character and capability to know and befriend God directly. Of course, an advocate can occasionally be helpful. If I were arrested, I would hire an attorney to represent my interests because I have scant knowledge of the legal system and how best to navigate it. If I were ill, I would hire a doctor to speed my healing. But I am perfectly capable of relating to God on my own, thank you very much. And so are you. Though we all can benefit from the spiritual insights of others, it is another thing entirely to suggest we need that person to mediate with God on our behalf due to some spiritual defect in us. Those who insist otherwise aren't so much interested in our redemption as in exercising power and control over the rest of us.

When I say that I am perfectly capable of relating to God on my own, I do not say that boastfully. I say it to affirm the spirit God has placed within me (and you), which makes this spiritual friendship possible. To assume a mediator, whether a priest or Jesus or a sacrament, is needed is to deny the great gift God has given each of us. We are perfectly equipped to be friends with God. No one need do something for us we are perfectly capable of doing for ourselves. No chasm exists that must be magically bridged by another more holy than ourselves. To insist otherwise is to deny our God-given capacity to draw near to God. Can professional clerics and rituals be useful? Yes. Are they required? Not at all, and sometimes they are even a hindrance. We can, in the words of a crusty Quaker I knew, "go to God ourselves." We have all the tools we need. Though it might be necessary to hone those tools, they are sufficient for the task.

Think of it. If a mediator were required in order to be in right relationship with God, how did those luckless souls born before Jesus and the church relate to God? If only Judaism provided that intercessory function, how did non-Jewish people enjoy a proper relationship with God? How have billions of people who've never heard of Judaism or Jesus or Muhammad approached God? And if such a mediator were essential, if God did require a mediating presence, then why wouldn't God have made that intercessor known to all people? What kind of God would insist on a mediator, then fail to make that mediator available to all?

Some Christians believe that rejecting the mediating role of Jesus is heretical. They're probably ready to burn this book right about now. They're entitled to their opinion, of course, but I part company with them on this theological point. From what we know of Jesus, and I'll be the first to say our historical knowledge of Jesus is scant, he appeared to be spiritually modest, claiming no unique power or authority for himself. People did not come to God *through* Jesus as much as they saw the priorities of God *in* Jesus. When our yes to God is as full and rich as Jesus's yes to God, then others will see the priorities of God in us, too.

So why has orthodox Christianity insisted God can be approached only through Jesus, that God can forgive only through the mediating presence of Jesus? Why did the church make this claim, especially when nothing Jesus did seems to support such a claim? Because as the church began interpreting the life of Jesus, they were simultaneously claiming to be the earthly representative of Jesus, which is a slick little trick if you can pull it off. Not only did the church claim to speak for Jesus but the Jesus they claimed to speak for seemed always to come down on the church's side, seemed always to affirm the church's priorities and values, seemed always to do the church's bidding.

This is the great temptation every religion faces—our all-too-human tendency to create theological systems that invariably place us in authority over others. It isn't because people in the church are evil or power mad, at least not most of us.* It is because every institution, whether political, religious, economic, or educational, seeks to extend its own reach and expand its advantages and interests. No matter how noble the principles

---

* I use the word *us* and not *them* when I speak about the church for a very important reason. I'm a part of the church, and have enjoyed the prestige and authority of the church all my life. To hold the church at arm's length after all these years, to deny my role and complicity in it, would be wrong. Further, I intend to remain in the church, helping the church become the community of Jesus I know it can become. This book is part of that effort.

are that birth an institution, it soon forsakes those principles to prolong and preserve itself. The perpetuity of the institution becomes the focus and goal.

How has the church done this? Many scholars would say it happened like this: First, we created language and rituals that supported our emerging community and made it seem as if those things had originated with Jesus. Stories were inserted in the earliest documents we shared with one another—a story of Jesus blessing a last supper in a way that closely resembled the emerging sacrament of communion, a story of Jesus calling Peter to leadership, thereby establishing a chain of authority that justified papal succession, early statements of faith that worked their way into the biblical text in which Jesus claimed to be "the way, the truth, and the life."

You do see the rule at work here, don't you? *Any religious institution placed in charge of its scripture will make sure that scripture justifies, protects, and preserves that institution.* We in the church are no different—no better, no worse. This isn't to cast aspersions on religious literature, only to remind us that we must approach such texts humbly, with eyes wide open, acutely aware that the letter can kill as quickly and cleanly as the sword.

This is why heresy has always been treated so harshly, not because it grieves God, as the church claimed, but because it undermines the authority of the church by chipping away at the foundation it had so carefully laid to establish its power. Because the penalty for heresy has been so harsh, it has discouraged theological and spiritual exploration, erecting a barrier around Christian expression we dared not cross. By inserting a middleman into a friendship God intended to be free and unencumbered, the church then controlled the conversation, extending divine intimacy and forgiveness to some, denying it to others. This in-or-out mentality is so foreign to anything we know about Jesus, it must be rejected as a human invention, not a divine revelation. We need no middleman, no advocate. We need no clerics threatening us with damnation if we dare question or disagree. We need only to trust that God is not a monster, and that we are not so grievously imperfect God cannot bear to befriend us. Of course, the theology of priestly intervention works only when we believe God's nature is inherently unforgiving. When we have confidence in God's grace, we won't devise systems of forgiveness and reconciliation. We will simply trust nothing can separate us from the love of God, then live with confidence and joy, unafraid for our future.

But there is a deeper problem with theologies of religious exclusivity and priestly power. They require that God be partial, that God play favorites. They require that God view some of her children as more loved, more deserving of status and mercy. In effect, they make God no better than the parent who so obviously favors one child that the others are scarred. In vesting some people with the power to mediate sin and confer forgiveness, God is comfortable leaving reconciliation up to the capricious whims of the human given that power.

And here let me offer an example. Two of my friends, both of them Catholic, divorced the same year. Both of the marriages had been brief, ending when their spouses were unfaithful. Both wished to participate in the sacrament of communion, but only one was permitted. The other was told by his priest he was in a state of sin and could not receive communion until his marriage was annulled. So a lifelong Catholic was denied the sacrament he most needed—the assurance of Christ's presence in and with him. He was, as you can imagine, devastated.

This is not a problem unique to Catholicism. It persists wherever grace, forgiveness, and reconciliation require human intercession, even if that grace depends upon the intercession of Jesus, which is itself a theological construct demanding our assent if we are to be forgiven. Even those Christians who insist no man has the power to mediate divine forgiveness nevertheless insist others must embrace their theology to be forgiven, as if their theology were not a human invention but something conceived in the rarefied air of heaven.

I used to believe in a God who vested certain persons with the power to forgive some people and condemn others. Now I believe God is unswervingly committed to the well-being of all people. I believe religious organizations, since the dawn of time, have usually sought to confine God's grace to those who share their ideology. Escaping their notice, I believe, is a God who pays no heed to such barriers but loves beyond them, bringing everyone to herself, as a hen gathers her chicks.

Why This Matters

When I interviewed to become the pastor of our Quaker meeting, a man on the search committee introduced himself as Dick and shook my hand, immediately putting me at ease with his kind demeanor. He didn't offer his last name, and I didn't ask it, but midway through the interview it occurred to me he had served for a number of years as the chief justice of our state's supreme court. After the interview, I asked him about this work, but he deftly changed the subject and asked about my children.

Until his death a decade later, he devoted many hours to our Quaker meeting, taking on some of the more unpleasant tasks others were reluctant to do. He seldom spoke about his position in state leadership, even when pressed. He seemed almost indifferent about his status, preferring instead to elevate others. He would often tell me I was the best pastor our Quaker meeting had ever had, though I later discovered he had told previous pastors the same thing. I wasn't upset, interpreting this as evidence of his desire to encourage others.

One evening, near the end of his life, I was visiting him in his home and asked him whether it was possible to tell if someone would be a good judge before they took office. He thought for a moment, then said, "We never really know until they put on the robe." That is, some people, when asked to judge others, do so humbly and equitably, careful to justly apply the rule of law to all. Other persons, after donning the robe, become arrogant, misusing their power to favor some and curse others. Some are mindful of the power invested in them and exercise that power carefully, while others handle it capriciously. It is almost impossible to know how power will affect those who hold it, until they hold it.

When the power to forgive is granted to a relative few, those few are more susceptible to arrogance, believing privilege is their due. When that power is coupled with a perceived divine authority, any misuse of power becomes especially harmful—to both the powerful and the powerless. Power must be tempered by wisdom, humility, and mercy. Absent those virtues, it will invariably tend toward self-aggrandizement and the abuse of others.

I've come to see the wisdom that my Quaker friend Dick brought to his civic duties. One's true character isn't often known until one is granted power. Should that power reveal a spirit of arrogance, it will be extraordinarily difficult to rescind that power, as the citizens in every political or religious dictatorship have learned. It is therefore up to us to create institutions and governments that promote dispersed and balanced power. This is especially true in the church, which wields a vast amount of cultural clout. When its leaders are unhealthy and self-serving, the contagion can't help but spread.

Winston Churchill, the irascible leader of Britain during the Second World War, said, "We shape our buildings, thereafter they shape us." That is also true of religion. The religious structures we create—and make no mistake, religions are born in the minds of people, not gods—in turn create us. The thoughtful assignment of power merits our most careful attention, lest we find ourselves harmed by those who treasure their authority over our well-being.

Chapter 4

God Needs Anger Management

First, I was told Jesus loved the little children,
Then I was told God was angry and it was my fault . . .

When one was raised in the One True Church, it was a rather easy matter, not to mention wonderfully convenient, to blame all the world's ills on other religions, which was why God had it out for them and was going to destroy them sooner or later, probably sooner. When I was an innocent child, which didn't last long, God wasn't mad at me, but once I was old enough to know better, once I knew enough not to sin but did anyway, then all bets were off, which the nuns told me happened when I was seven years old and had reached what the Catholics called the "age of reason." After that, I was expected to join the One True Church, take communion, keep my nose clean, and avoid God's wrath. That the leaders of the church, all of them childless, believed seven-year-olds are capable of complex moral reasoning says something about their inexperience.

The Baptist church my sister attended cut kids a little more slack. Their pastor talked about the "age of accountability," which he said was thirteen, giving Baptist kids six more years of scot-free sinning, which might have been why my sister jumped ship to the Baptists. Of course, once you turned thirteen, you were under intense pressure to be baptized, join the church, and not sin any longer, even though the Baptist preacher said not sinning is impossible, which is why God despises us, since God is holy and hates sin and can't bear to look at us, just like I couldn't bear to be around Jerry Sipes, who never brushed his teeth or took a shower.

"We are as filthy rags to God," the Baptist minister told us the Sunday I visited his church. Though he said "we," I had the distinct feeling he wasn't including himself. Now that I'm a pastor, I totally get that, and often say "we" when what I really mean is "everyone in the room but me."

He went on to say our mere existence is an affront to God, given our sinful natures, and that committing one teensy sin, like telling someone she doesn't need to lose weight even though she does, is as bad as murdering a million people. This made me think that even trying to be nice to overweight people would be a sin, causing God to hate me. My sister was a bit pudgy at the time, certainly not fat, but a little thick in the ankles, so I thought of pointing that out to her in an effort to be truthful and stay on God's good side, except that the pastor told us we couldn't help but sin, that even if we tried to be good, we couldn't. We needed Jesus, who was sinless, to stand before God on our behalf so God wouldn't pitch us headfirst into hell.

I was thirteen, just entering the age of accountability, when I first heard this and supposed it to be true since the pastor sounded so confident. Sitting in the pew, weighing whether or not to tell my sister to lose a pound or two, I decided to give my heart to Jesus, though I had no idea what that meant. The pastor urged us to come forward and repent of our sins, but I repented quietly in the pew, even though the pastor said that wasn't good enough.

"Whosoever shall deny me before men, him will I also deny before my Father which is in heaven," he said.

It wasn't that I was denying Jesus, I just didn't feel the need to bother people with a public announcement. Plus, I was a bit of an introvert, which I hoped God might understand, he having made me that way, and my family wasn't given to dramatic proclamations. We believed in working quietly behind the scenes. So I asked God to forgive me if I had angered him, and promised to try harder, which I did for the rest of the time we were at the Baptist church. I was nice to my sister, dropped a dollar in the offering plate, and shook the pastor's hand at the back door, telling him I enjoyed his sermon, even though it had scared the bejeezus out of me.

There must have been a general conspiracy among the churches in our town to scare the teenagers, because I began hearing more about the age of accountability. Some of my friends started attending youth group, gathering in homes on Sunday evenings to be terrified. It turned out God was opposed to everything we wanted to do, and not just mildly opposed but over-the-top enraged at our teenage inclinations. If

God had been a person, we would have sent him to anger management classes.

We were taught that in a fit of rage God killed every human except Noah and his family but weren't told that God pledged never to do it again (Genesis 8:21). Probably because the sign of God's pledge was the rainbow, which suggests God is more kindly disposed toward homosexuals than we've been led to believe.

It never seemed to occur to the people warning us about God's anger that no sane person would want to be in a relationship with the deity they described.

"Let me get this right," I wanted to say. "You want me to give my heart to someone who is offended by my mere existence, someone I must appease with a weekly confession of my failures and shortcomings?"

I once heard a woman say God was like the man your parents warned you never to marry. Then the church came along and said you'd be miserable without him. If, after listening to the god they described, you decided your life would be just fine without him, the church went berserk.

"How can you reject God?" they'd ask, incredulous, then demand you reconsider. "Don't you know that God loves you?"

The church kept at it until you caved in, just to get them off your back and make your grandmother happy.

But sometimes even the church realized they'd gone too far with the God-as-monster motif, so they told you about Jesus, who loved everyone, especially children, which made you feel better about things, until they told you he was also God. Then you were thoroughly confused, but fortunately it was time to move from home and go to college, where you became an atheist because not believing in the God you'd been told about seemed somehow more sensible and gracious. Except when you came home for Thanksgiving, you let it slip that you maybe didn't believe in God anymore and your mother cried and your father said, "What do you mean, you don't believe in God? What kind of crap are they teaching you? I'm not paying them to teach you that!" So you had to leave college and get a job at Walmart and it ruined your life, all because of the lousy theological education you had received at the hands of the church.

But all that lay over the horizon in your future. Long before you went to college, you stayed up nights worrying that you had offended God and he would zap you in your sleep.* The pastors were certainly no help, telling stories each Sunday about young people who had died suddenly, without knowing Jesus, and were at that moment roasting in hell, which was no doubt a great comfort to those parents who had lost children. When I was young, a boy in our town drowned, and even though he was a good kid and went to church every Sunday, the pastors weren't inclined to pass up a wonderful opportunity and admitted to some uncertainty about his place of residence.

"Shall that boy's death be in vain?" they asked, as if it had been the boy's idea all along to die and serve as an object lesson for the rest of us.

Our town's churches were nothing if not efficient, utilizing

---

* Whenever I think of God zapping someone, it somehow seems more appropriate to use the pronoun *he*.

every misfortune to scare us into faith. In early April 1974, a swirl of tornadoes tore across the Midwest, much to the delight of some Christians in our town, who dangled the 319 fatalities before us for months. The tornadoes, they believed, were a sure sign of God's anger with America. God was mad about abortion, homosexuality, sex, liberals, communists . . . all the usual suspects. While God was furious about very specific things, the deaths were rather indiscriminate. Toddlers who'd never had abortions or sex or even a vague liberal thought were killed just as handily as the most enthusiastic sinners. But then logic wasn't the governing theme of their theology, which was mostly interested in making sure God hated the same things they hated, and punished the same people they would have punished were it not for America's pesky Constitution.

These theological assertions were made to defend God's goodness and power in the midst of evil. Why do bad things happen to good people if God is all-loving, all-knowing, and all-powerful? These explanations are called *theodicies*, if you care to know the technical term, and we've been creating them since it first occurred to us there might be a god. Naturally, shortly after God's existence occurred to us, we hurried to define God's character, then defended our definition of God by explaining away the very problem we had hoped God would protect us from, namely the problem of evil.

It's an easy matter to explain away the presence of evil when it's visited upon evil people. We tell ourselves they have been given their just deserts, that God loves justice, and is setting matters right. It is the suffering of the innocent and blameless that stymies us. Why does God allow the innocent to suffer? Why are children killed by tornadoes? Why are babies born with birth defects? Why did we get Donald Trump as our president?

The church of my childhood said our suffering was a mystery. They told me the ways of the Lord were too mysterious to understand and I would drive myself crazy dwelling on such matters. Since I belonged to the One True Church, they couldn't very well say I was in the wrong denomination or religion, so that option was off the table. The church has always been loath to admit to ignorance, so it often falls back on the distant cousin of ignorance, mystery.

The ways of the Lord are not for us to understand.
We'll understand it better by and by.
Who are we to question God?
God's ways are not our ways.

Later, when I became an evangelical, evil was blamed on our personal shortcomings. There was no such thing as innocence. All had sinned and fallen short of the glory of God. Some evangelicals I knew pitched the doctrine of the age of accountability right out the window, swearing up and down that even newborn infants have a sinful nature, deserving whatever misfortune befalls them. This sinful nature had its roots in Adam and Eve, who had apparently sinned so spectacularly we were still paying off their debt, lo these many years later. But seriously, how healthy can any religion be that begins with the premise that babies are stained with guilt? I've met some seven-year-olds who make me wish birth control were retroactive, but can we stop picking on babies?

I have a friend whose mother was a drug addict, so he had

to go live with his mother's parents, who, when he did something wrong, made him stand in a corner for hours at a time apologizing to God for what he had done. I used to be judgmental about drug addicts, but now I totally understand why my friend's mom took drugs, which I thought showed remarkable restraint, given how lousy her life must have been with parents like that. That appears to be the best some people can do with their Christianity—make a kid stand in the corner for hours at a time pleading with God and shaking with fear. But if that is what Christianity is all about, I'd prefer to be a pagan.

Don't you wish people had to pass a test before they could reproduce, and that the first question on the test was "Do you believe infants have a sinful nature?" The answer would tell us gobs about their mental and emotional well-being. What child, constantly reminded of her faults and failures, could grow up to become a whole and happy adult? Ironically, the adults who foist this theology on children often do so out of a deep concern for their children's well-being, seldom realizing they are making their children's lives a fresh and living hell.

It's long past time we change our thinking about God, human nature, and evil. Perhaps we suffer not because we're inherently evil but because God lacks the power to prevent human suffering. Perhaps God is all-loving and actually wants the very best for everyone but can't intervene in time and space to make that happen. Or maybe God isn't all-loving so purposely manipulates events to ensure our misery. Or maybe God lacks awareness of the future so is unable to foresee the calamity fate might heap upon us.

When faced with those possibilities, I chose to believe God

is all-loving, but lacks the power and foreknowledge to create a world free of evil. The alternative, it seemed to me, was to believe in an all-powerful, all-knowing God whose motives are unloving, which is no alternative at all. Can you imagine a force let loose in the world that holds all the power and knowledge there is to hold but does not exercise that power and knowledge with love? Power and knowledge not informed by love are the hallmarks of every tyrant the world has known.

I have heard people say, "I wouldn't want to live in a world God didn't control." But if God is all-loving, if love is God's primary virtue, that same love can help us bear the evil and suffering we experience. *I would rather God have love and lack power, than have power and lack love, for love can remedy the absence of power, but power can never compensate for the absence of love.*

Nor am I so driven to explain away all suffering and evil that I would lay it at the feet of some pretended inherent human evil. I will not ascribe the trait of evil to all of humanity just to tie my theology in a neat little bow. Evil and suffering are real parts of life, adequately explained by the vagaries of nature and the moral inconsistency of humanity. This is not to say all humans are evil or morally broken, but those who choose evil inflict great damage on others. So to assign my three-year-old granddaughter the same weight of sin one would assign Hitler is ridiculous, and makes the church's teaching of original or inherent sin absurd.

One of my earliest memories of my mother happened late one night when I was around five years old. It was well past midnight, and I awoke and walked into my parents' bedroom to find Mom mending my clothes. Years later, when I read in the third chapter of Genesis about God making clothes for Adam and Eve, I thought of my mother and realized how much her kindness had shaped my vision of God.

If there is a god, and that god judges us, either now or at our deaths, then that judgment is tempered with love. We need not fear a penalty imposed upon us for the mere sake of our humanity. God is not an angry father, beating his children into submission. God is a mother, sewing clothes for her children late into the night.

Why It Matters

One summer day when I was around twelve, I knocked on a friend's door, hoping he could play. When he answered, I saw a welt in the shape of a hand on his face and I could tell he was upset. He hurried past me, climbed on his bicycle, and rode away. I followed him, hurrying to keep up, until he pulled over underneath a tree a few blocks from his home, flung his bike to the ground, and began stalking around the tree.

"I hate my dad," he said. "I wish he'd die."

"What did your dad do?" I asked. I remember being upset by the intensity of his emotion.

"The son of a bitch hit me again."

This was new territory for me. I had never heard someone my age refer to his father that way, and had never known a father to strike his child on the face. I had been the recipient of several swats on the bottom, but my parents had never slapped me or my siblings. I wasn't sure what to say. After a few minutes my friend settled down and we never discussed the matter again, but from time to time I would see a bruise on his arm or face and wonder if he had been beaten again.

The family eventually moved away, but thirty-some years later I received a letter from my friend's father, taking me to task for a book I had written about grace. God, he informed me, was a jealous, angry god. He cited several Bible verses, then closed the letter by urging me to repent before God destroyed me. I recalled his abuse of his son many years before so wasn't surprised to learn the god he worshipped was similarly predisposed toward violence.

Wrathful gods create wrathful followers. Any effort toward peace that doesn't take into account the corrosive effect of wrathful religion is bound to fail, for it ignores the emotions and beliefs that fuel hatred and division. This is one of the greatest challenges facing humanity—the disproportionate power of a relative few to distort and destroy human community. We must move beyond the common mantra that all religious traditions and expressions are equally beneficial. That is simply not true. Some beliefs breed violence, others peace. The god we worship will lead us to life or death. It is up to us to choose the god we affirm.

Chapter 5

———

The Best Deal Ever

I was scarcely out of the womb when my parents took me to St. Mary's Queen of Peace and had Father McLaughlin sprinkle me with holy water in the event I died before I reached the age of reason. It simply wouldn't do for me to get hit by a car at the age of five and go straight to hell, or Purgatory, a layover stop on the way to hell, where I could board the plane to heaven if enough people prayed for me. Though I must admit that when I first heard of Purgatory, I was strangely attracted to it. Hell sounded miserable—hot and humid and irritating. Heaven seemed too sweet, full of people like my grandmother whose idea of a good time was praying the rosary. Purgatory sounded just right, like the baby bear's porridge in "Goldilocks and the Three Bears."

My parents didn't ask me whether I wanted to be baptized, and since I wasn't talking at the time, I would have been hardpressed to tell them my preference. Still, it would have been nice to have been asked. I was dozing in my mother's arms, warm and content, when a strange man took me from her, threw water in my face, and jabbered at me in Latin, not a word of which I understood. Had I known I was being saved from hell for the next seven years, I might have been more receptive to the idea, but I'm told I greeted my salvation with sobbing.

Though I didn't realize it at the time, had I died, it would have been the best deal I'd ever made—a moment of slight discomfort for a potential eternity of heaven. It was like dying after making only one monthly payment on a million-dollar insurance policy. Such a deal! Unfortunately, I was never able to collect on it, remaining in robust health throughout my childhood, so the water in my face did me little good. It did seem to please my parents, however, so in that regard was beneficial.

The baptism was intended to carry me through the choppy waters of childhood, until I could decide for myself whether I wished to join the One True Church and go to heaven. Even then, my parents decided for me.

When I turned seven, my mother informed me that it was time to take classes and receive my first communion.

"What if I find religious rituals meaningless and don't wish to participate?" I asked.

Actually, I didn't say that. I said okay, because this was back in the old days and we didn't argue with our parents.

So I found myself in a class with thirty or so other kids where we were told receiving first communion would change our lives forever and that if we went to confession and Mass every week, we'd slide through the pearly gates like greased pigs when we died. Naturally, I signed on. Who wouldn't want such a deal? Millions, as it turns out, who preferred the even easier route of accepting Jesus as their Savior, getting baptized, and going to heaven no matter what they did afterward.

"Once saved, always saved," Jerry Sipes told me, when we were in the eighth grade.

"You mean you could accept Jesus as your Savior, then go murder a bunch of people and have sex before you get married, and you'll still go to heaven when you die?" I asked, incredulous.

"Just because you broke your word, doesn't mean God breaks his," Jerry said.

You can imagine my elation at discovering the best deal the church has ever offered anyone! I felt as if I had walked into Kroger's the day they were handing out free Hostess Twinkies.

"You mean I can accept Jesus as my Savior, and do whatever I want, and still go to heaven when I die?" I asked again, just to be sure.

"That's right," Jerry Sipes said, triumphantly. "Ain't it great!"

So I went through first communion and confessed my sins each week and attended Mass, just in case the Catholics were right, and when I was in the ninth grade, under Jerry Sipes's expert guidance, I also got myself saved, just in case he was right. In all the years I had known Jerry Sipes, he had never been right about anything, but getting saved was such an easy matter, I saw no harm in doing it.

"First, you have to admit you're a sinner," Jerry told me.

Easy enough.

"Then you have to believe Jesus was perfect and died the death you deserved," he said.

That seemed reasonable.

"Then you have to say a prayer accepting Jesus as your Savior," Jerry said.

"Okay, I did."

"That's it. Now you're saved!" Jerry said, wildly excited for me. "How does it feel?"

To be honest, I felt no different than before I was saved, which caused me to assume I had already been saved by the One True Church, but I didn't want to disappoint Jerry, so I told him I'd never felt better, then thanked him for getting me saved. I was the tenth person he'd saved in as many days, so he won a free week at church camp, where he lost his virginity but still got to go to heaven when he died. Or so he said, but he's not dead yet, so we can't be sure.

It was right about then I began toying with the idea of becoming a pastor and helping people go to heaven when they died, but I also wanted to be a forest ranger and couldn't make up my mind. As the years went on, I began to wonder if Jerry Sipes had overpromised, and that a right relationship with God was a bit more nuanced than Jerry had let on. I also began to notice how some Christians, I won't say which ones, tended to reduce complex matters to the simplest terms, framing their world in a way that required the least human effort. A simple prayer guarantees an eternal life of blessing. God created the world in six days. Everything, including our human transformation, happens with a quick snap of the fingers. Accept Jesus, and he'll change you in the blink of an eye.

Now, I don't doubt some people have experienced radical, near-instantaneous conversions. I've heard their testimonies, and maybe you have, too. But my experience is different. In both my experience and my understanding, spiritual change and growth most often unfold over time.

It only makes sense: Spiritual growth, like physical growth, is difficult, and the work of a lifetime. It tends to be gradual, slowly unfolding, with two steps forward and one step back. The Genesis story of God creating the world in six days holds such appeal partly because it confirms our hope for easy transformation and instant salvation, despite evidence that God clearly seems willing to let creation unfold gradually, even glacially. That it's taken Earth some 4.6 billion years to get where it is today suggests God might be more patient than some religious folk would have us believe.

I recently met a kind, older man who had spent his life counseling and teaching at a high school and college. As we were talking, I sensed he was one of those inspirational individuals we've all known and appreciated. He mentioned he'd grown up in the church and had wanted to be a pastor, but when he met with a committee from his denomination to discuss the matter, they refused to recommend him for ministry because he couldn't tell them the specific date he'd been saved.

Though he had grown up in the church and had participated in its programs since early childhood, because he had not had an identifiable moment of salvation, he was excluded from ministry.

I thought how ironic it was that he would have been welcomed in church leadership if he had spent his youth and early adulthood abusing drugs, bullying people smaller than or different from himself, cheating, lying, and stealing, then had attended a revival, gotten saved, and a week later appeared before the same committee, able to name the specific date of his salvation. Oh, how the gates of the church would have swung open to welcome him into leadership! If you think I'm exaggerating, I will tell you I have seen it happen time and again.

But let a person grow up in the bosom of a faith community, let that person be trained since infancy in the loving ways of Jesus, let that person know nothing except love, acceptance, kindness, and wisdom, if he is unable to name a specific day of salvation, he will—at least in many churches I've known—be judged unqualified to lead or teach others.

I would not dismiss out of hand the other applicant's suitability for ministry, but neither would I hasten to affirm his fitness for leadership. Instead, I would express thanks that he seemed to have experienced a significant encounter with God, then I would explain that before he could be trusted with leadership, we would need further evidence of his transformation. I would want to know he was in it for the long haul. I would want to see how he conducted himself in a variety of situations, and whether he seemed committed to life in a spiritual community. I would want him to study and read and reflect. I would offer to meet with him regularly to discuss our shared faith, and would hope he had something to teach me. But I would ultimately insist that one significant moment with God is rarely sufficient proof of an entirely changed life. It might well be the beginning of a changed life, but more time would be needed to discern even that.

In other words, I would suggest to him that spiritual growth and maturity are evolutionary, not revolutionary.

When we married, my wife and I needed a kitchen table. I decided I could save money by building one, so I went to the lumberyard, bought several pine boards, and made a table. While it looked handsome, and my wife assured me I was a genius, my table lacked strength and lasted only a few years before collapsing. My grandfather, an experienced woodworker, surveyed the ruin and said, "You should have used cherry boards. I thought about telling you that when you made it, but figured you should learn that lesson yourself."

My grandfather was maddening that way, freely dispensing unsolicited advice but hesitant to speak when guidance was most needed.

The reason cherry is superior to pine for furniture making is that it grows more slowly. As a result, the wood is stronger and more enduring than pine.

This is no less true of spiritual growth. Lessons learned easily and quickly seldom stick, leaving us disheartened. This is why the promise of instant holiness is ultimately discouraging; we are promised a transformation that for most people doesn't last.

In my teens, as I became more theologically curious, evangelicalism was undergoing a revival in the United States. Its influence showed up in many churches, including the Quaker meeting I was then attending. I was attracted by the vitality, certainty, and community I found among evangelicals and quickly joined their tribe. I spent nearly every evening at Bible studies sponsored by different churches and groups, where I was universally assured that if I accepted Jesus as my Savior, my life would immediately and dramatically change. So I did, and for a while it worked, as it usually did whenever I accepted Jesus, something I did a lot in those days. But then the new would wear off, and I would return to some of my old habits, despite the evangelicals' assurances that I was a new man. My old habits weren't all that bad—I wasn't robbing banks or selling secrets to the communists—but being a teenage male, I had several impure thoughts each hour I couldn't seem to help. I remember feeling I had let God down, suspecting that of the 1.5 billion Christians in the world, I was the worst one.

Around that same time, I was invited to a revival at another church, where the speaker, I'm not making this up, had been a member of the Mafia. He regaled us for nearly an hour with stories from his colorful past, causing most of the males present to wish they, too, had belonged to the Mafia. He kept saying how unhappy he had been back then, but for someone who'd been unhappy he seemed remarkably cheerful when telling about it. Then the man said he was sent to prison, where he had found the Lord and gotten saved. There must have been a clock in the room where he was saved, because he named the precise moment it happened, causing the pastor to almost faint dead away.

"Imagine that," he said, interrupting the Mafia man, "remembering the exact second you were saved! We should all be able to do that!"

Even though I hadn't been saved all that long, at least that time around, I couldn't remember the specific date and wished I had written it down on a slip of paper and tucked it in my wallet so I could retrieve it if I were ever asked.

"Oh, yes, I've been saved. On, let's see," I would say, reaching for my wallet and unfolding the piece of paper, "yes, here it is, October fifth, 1976."

I'm making up October 5. I actually can't remember, so I hope God doesn't expect me to know the precise date, though I'm pretty sure it was 1976. I got saved so often back then, it's hard to know.

But it was what the Mafia man said after naming the precise second of his salvation that discouraged me most of all.

"And after I got saved," he said, "I was never tempted to sin again. I just walked away from it and left it all behind."

Instead of leaving the revival hopeful, thinking the Christian life was a real possibility for me, I left disheartened, convinced I hadn't actually been saved since I seemed incapable of the holiness he described. I wish someone had spoken after him, someone who might have told us the spiritual life doesn't usually work that way, that we often continue to wrestle with darkness. I hadn't read the Bible enough to know about Paul's "thorn in the flesh." I hadn't reflected on the wilderness temptations of Jesus, and how the very nature of temptations meant Jesus risked succumbing to them.

It isn't an easy matter to overcome our failed attempts at holiness, especially when so many Christians continue to insist we can be instantly transformed. So for us the spiritual life consists primarily of guilt and recrimination, which we are embarrassed to admit, so don't seek help or counsel from persons more experienced than ourselves, not wanting them to think poorly of us. In fact, I believe the perception of failed spirituality, and its accompanying feelings of guilt and self-blame, is a leading cause of persons leaving Christian community. After all, why would we persist in a lifestyle we've convinced ourselves we're unsuited for?

When I became more intentional about the Christian faith, in my late teens, I was quite pleased with myself for being so spiritually pure. Then I went on a date with a young woman I admired, and my purity, which I had thought unimpeachable, was tarnished. Disappointed in myself, I stopped attending meeting for worship, believing I was no longer fit to be in Christian community. I suppose it was a self-shunning. I stayed away for nearly a year before confiding in a seasoned Quaker, who pointed out that Christian transformation is a lifelong process, that I would have moments of holy obedience and moments of weakness. I keep having to remind myself of that.

I am happy for those persons who were saved at a specific moment and never again felt the tug of sin and struggle. But I suspect such people are rare, and far fewer in number than the church would have us believe. As for me, I am not saved, if by saved we mean a perfect state of faith and holiness made possible by our relationship with Jesus. At one time, I thought I was saved, but I was mistaken, simply affirming a theology I accepted with little thought. Today, I would say I am *being* saved, that each day presents its spiritual and ethical challenges, some of which I meet, some of which I don't. Being saved is, without a doubt, the hardest work I have ever undertaken. There are moments in my journey toward salvation that are exquisite and filled with joy, and there are moments of great despair, when I question everything I have taught, and been taught. There are days when I am so frustrated with my Christian life I would happily leave it behind, and days I treasure it more than life itself. Through it all I know this: I am not saved. Not yet. But I am being saved. I am moving toward wholeness and life and love. The arc of my life is pointing toward salvation, and that is enough.

Why It Matters

Now let's get to the heart of the matter. What does it say about God when we believe people are changed in an instant? Doesn't it suggest God is impatient, unable to persist with us as we grow? After all, what kind of parents would insist their child be instantly transformed? What spouse would demand instant perfection from his or her mate? Why this emphasis on immediate change? Are we celebrating the power of God or are we revealing our own impatience with the often glacial pace of spiritual maturity?

God is patient. God is kind. And so must we be, not just with others but with ourselves, patiently trusting God is working in us, perfecting us, assisting us in our journey. With so able a guide, there is no reason to despair when we move backwards. How else can we learn? "Success," Abraham Lincoln said, "is a poor teacher."* We learn in our setbacks and are honed and

---

* At least I thought Abraham Lincoln said it. But when I looked it up on Google, it attributed the saying to a Robert Kiyosaki, who wrote a book called *Rich Dad Poor Dad* that sold a zillion copies. Donald Trump praised the book, which made me suspicious of Robert Kiyosaki, even though I still think it's true that success is a poor teacher. If Abraham Lincoln didn't say it first, he should have.

perfected by our failures. Failures and setbacks teach us what success and perfection can't. In our spiritual failures, we learn humility, thereby avoiding self-righteousness, the cancer of the soul.

As I said earlier, I have heard Christians claim to be instantly transformed and perfected, and while I don't think they're dishonest, I do believe they lack self-awareness. Therefore, let us confirm what we know from our experience to be true—God is devoted to our loving growth, not our sterile perfection.

Chapter 6

I Was Pleased to Discover God and I Hated the Same Things

When I was in the sixth grade, a For Sale sign went up at the Swansons' house across the street from us. Eddie Swanson, like all boys, had a little voice in his head that warned him when he was on the verge of doing something stupid, but like the rest of us, Eddie totally ignored it, so I thoroughly enjoyed his company. When the Swansons moved, I was devastated. My mother, sensing my distress, told me that God never closes a door without opening a window, a thought that cheered me immensely. I began praying that the window God would open would have something to do with girls moving in next door, more specifically, the girls on *Petticoat Junction*—Billie Jo, Bobbie Jo, and Betty Jo—who struck me as ideal neighbors.

In the inscrutable way of the Divine, my prayers went unanswered and a new family bought the Swansons' house. They had two boys near my age, who were forbidden by their religion from wearing shorts, so the thing I remember most about them was their sweat. They were, and remain, the dampest people I ever knew. They also attended church four times a week, which seemed excruciating to me. I could barely endure Saturday night confession and Sunday morning Mass, but they slogged through church twice on Sunday, and once each on Wednesday and Friday. It wasn't a fifty-minute-and-out church service, either. They went on for hours, whooping and hollering and praying and singing and speaking in tongues and probably handling snakes and drinking battery acid for all I knew.

This was back in the days when Catholics wouldn't be caught dead in a Protestant church, so when our neighbors invited my brother, David, to visit their church and our mother said okay, I was shocked. Then again, there were five of us kids, and a 20 percent reduction in parenting, if only for a few hours, was a godsend and might have kept our parents from killing and eating us. So my brother went and was gone for three hours and returned home terrified, his eyes rolled back in his head. He lay in bed for three days, staring at the ceiling and babbling incoherently, obviously suffering from what I now recognize as post-traumatic stress disorder.

Eventually, David was able to tell us what had happened.

"They were running up and down the aisle and one guy ran from the back of the church to the front of the church on the backs of the pews. Then they took me down front to the pastor and he prayed at me, then they beat on drums and played guitars, and told me to stop wearing shorts and join their church."

Apparently, their entire religion hinged on men not wearing shorts, due to some obscure verse in the Bible having to do with men not dressing like women, which seemed to suggest the women in their church wore shorts, but they didn't, either. They dressed like pioneer women. I wouldn't have been surprised to see a Conestoga wagon parked outside their house with oxen grazing on the lawn. The women couldn't cut their hair, and the men had to wear theirs like Sergeant Carter on *Gomer Pyle*, which our neighbor boys snuck over to watch every afternoon since they weren't allowed to own a television, either.

"Television is a sin," the older one said during a commercial break.

"And so is wearing shorts," added his little brother, who pointed this out at every opportunity.

"Let's watch *The Partridge Family* after this," the older suggested.

Their religion placed so many restrictions on behavior, I couldn't keep track of them. No TV, no movies, no shorts, no swimming, no dancing, no card playing, no men having long hair, no women having short hair, no marrying outside the church, no women speaking in church, no divorce, no sports, no college, no casual dating, no makeup, no jewelry. Now that I think about it, they were kind of like the Amish, but with cars, and none of the charm.

Occasionally I will hear someone sigh wistfully and say, "Wouldn't it be nice to be Amish? Their lives seem so simple and happy." But I don't know anyone who observed the brand of Christianity our neighbors practiced and said, "That's the religion for me!"

Knowing they wouldn't be able to entice anyone to join

their church, they encouraged those already in it to have as many kids as possible. I never got an accurate head count of our neighbors' children; there were simply too many of them. It was like trying to count salmon swimming upstream. One could only count the number in a given area and extrapolate.

Despite the music and the general frenzy, there seemed so little joy in their religion. And so little purpose. God's desires seemed so trivial, appeased by someone's strict adherence to a religious code that, even when strictly followed, didn't measurably improve the world. What cosmic catastrophe was avoided by short hair? How was the world improved by wearing long pants? What danger was averted by the absence of makeup? To be fair, I can't see that my eating fish on Friday did much to improve the world, either.

Who made this stuff up? What person, in response to the question *How can we best please God?* arrived at these answers? Why was God content with so little? It seemed like such a meager response when so much more was needed. How, in the face of staggering human need, could a reasonable person believe that what God wanted most of all was for women not to wear jewelry?

I don't know how to say this without sounding judgmental and self-righteous, qualities that usually nauseate me, but these kinds of religious expressions strike me as paper thin. I never sense an "at-peaceness" about them. They have the form of religion but none of the spirit, none of the delight, awe, compassion, or insight. Looking back on my neighbors' religion, it seemed like a bunch of guys formed a church that would ensure their hold on power, their wives' submission, and their fondness for the 1950s. Of course, we are experts at cloaking our preferences in religious language, making it sound as if they were God's idea, then measuring our devotion to God by our commitment to those same preferences. It's like starting a religion based on our love for chocolate, then being pleased with ourselves and feeling holy whenever we eat chocolate. Beware of any religion that never asks anything of us we aren't already regularly doing.

This religious tendency toward legalism is as old as religion itself. Years later, I studied the history of religion and learned that the rules in the Book of Leviticus were referred to as *holiness codes*. Though many Jewish people no longer feel bound by them, that hasn't kept us Christians from composing our own holiness codes. Indeed, they can be found in almost every religion to varying degrees. Most often, holiness codes are used to signal a "separateness" from the world. My neighbors didn't dress like anyone else in our neighborhood. We could tell at a glance they weren't Methodists or Catholics or Presbyterians. I still find it instructive that whenever I see someone peculiarly dressed, more often than not they are motivated by religious principles.

Others might find such distinctions helpful—I've been told they remind the wearers of their spiritual obligations—but I'm wary, not to mention weary, of religion that calls attention to itself by attire. Seriously, if your faith is so easily forgotten it takes clothing to remind you of it, then maybe you're not all that committed to your faith. I've also heard proponents of holiness codes say their clothing safeguards modesty, but have you ever noticed how the burden of the codes weighs most heavily upon the women? Do men have so little self-control that women must conceal every curve lest males be led astray?

If so, that is a male problem best solved by self-discipline, not by placing further restrictions upon women.

When I first learned about holiness codes, I wondered why they were so widespread, especially those rules that pertain to our attire. Why do priests wear Roman collars? Why do nuns wear habits? Why do Sikh men wear turbans? Why do Muslim women wear head coverings? Why couldn't my childhood neighbors wear shorts? Why did early Quakers dress in gray? Why do some Jewish men wear small boxes called frontlets on their foreheads and grow their hair into sidelocks? Why do Mormons wear temple undergarments? Why do certain Pentecostal women wear their hair in buns? Why do Buddhist monks wear distinctive robes? Why do televangelists have big hair?

Of course, some of these customs are rooted in history or scriptures and have become meaningful traditions to those who practice them. But—you knew there would be a *but*—it seems clear that the emphasis on holiness codes often supplants the message of the founder. Which likely means that at some point in the evolution of many religions, *looking* like a disciple became more important than *being* a disciple. It is this shift from *being* to *looking like* I find unsettling, for it invariably leads to self-righteousness when one becomes a little too pleased with one's own devotion and a little too judgmental about the devotion of others.* Kind of like I'm being now, for instance.

---

* A Quaker couple were leaving the meetinghouse one Sunday after worship. The husband turned to his wife and said, "Dear, I do believe we were the plainest Friends at meeting today."

In my own tradition, early Quakers who violated the dress codes were first visited by unsmiling elders and reminded why buttons and lapels were evil. If they failed to heed the elders' counsel and persisted in their wickedness, they were shown the door. This is the dark side of holiness: it inevitably excludes.

Several times a week I receive letters or e-mails from persons describing mistreatment they've suffered at the hands of the church, usually for a perceived sin or violation. Perhaps they had been divorced, or had decided to be born gay, or had drunk a beer in public.* One woman was kicked to the curb for wearing pants, another was shunned for leaving her abusive husband after their pastor ordered her to remain with him. Another family was asked to leave their church after reporting an incident of molestation in the church to the legal authorities. All of these were considered violations of their churches' religious codes.

Why do so many people of faith emphasize obedience to rules and codes at the expense of mercy? And why do we tend to reduce the mystery, awe, and wonder of God to a checklist of obscure regulations that have little bearing on our spiritual growth? When one considers the vast complexity of the universe and the Spirit we believe set it in motion, why have we assumed that same Spirit cares so deeply about clothing, church authority, and gender roles? Why do we emphasize the mundane in a world of such magnificence?

---

* Don't send me a letter telling me gays didn't decide to be born that way. I know that. I'm employing hyperbole, a favorite tool of writers everywhere.

When I was a Catholic, participating each week in confession, I remember telling Father McLaughlin I had eaten meat on Friday. The Vietnam War was raging, children were being burnt to death by napalm, America's cities were aflame, Martin Luther King, Jr., and Bobby Kennedy had been assassinated, and I had to ask God's forgiveness for eating a hamburger. How had eating fish on Fridays become the measure of holiness?

People obsessed with religious legalese talk about how rare and difficult true holiness is, when it is so easy compared to the depth of transformed living Jesus called for. It's much simpler to wear the right clothes, eat the right food, and wear the right hairstyle than it is to love mercy and do justice. No wonder so many people have reduced religion to these simple, attainable standards. It is this settling for so little that poses such a threat to spirituality. It creates a faith so puddle-shallow, it dries up quickly. This is likely why religions that emphasize the trivial fail to produce the fresh thought necessary for spiritual renewal and rejuvenation. Unable to produce a Meister Eckhart or John Woolman, a Joan Chittister or Richard Rohr, they become mired in the tired expressions of the past. This is why in order to grow spiritually, people must sometimes leave their religion. Of course, when they do, they are warned their souls are in jeopardy, when just the opposite is true. They are, perhaps for the first time in their lives, experiencing a freshness of spirit made possible by their departure.

It seems counterintuitive that in order to flourish spiritually we might be called to leave our church. Our tendency is to double down, to follow the holiness codes more zealously than we had. I knew a woman who had been raised in a theologically rigid church. In her early twenties, she experienced a spiritual disconnect from her childhood faith, though she found it nearly impossible to leave. She succeeded in leaving her home church only by finding another one equally inflexible. Eventually, however, she was able to leave that church and not attend anywhere for several years. It was in this time of "desert" that she began reading widely, conversing with others from different faiths, and drawing near to God. Today, she participates in a progressive Episcopal church, where she found permission to think and explore.

Though it took me only a handful of sentences to write of her spiritual transition, in practice it was much more difficult. We often struggle to be free from the grasp of rigid religion, and just as many fail as succeed. I once knew a man who reasoned that if beginning each day reading the Bible was good, then reading the Bible all day long was even better. Of course, he couldn't do this and still work, so he soon lost his job. Eventually, he succeeded in alienating his family and friends and ended up in an inpatient facility for the mentally ill. I know this isn't the outcome for all who are religiously diligent, but it does seem to me that the especially scrupulous do become unhealthily obsessed, losing sight of the true values of life.

If rigid, rules-based religion can kill one's spirit, can it ever be helpful? In a few instances, I have met persons whose moral compasses were so askew the only thing making them fit for society was their fear of God's punishment. For them, the carefully defined restraints of religion, with its strict codes and consequences, kept them from harming others. Unable to self-regulate, they required rigid religion to check their impulse toward violence. This might be why fundamentalist religions tend to flourish in prisons.

I was once invited to give a talk at a prison by a chaplain who had read an essay I had written and incorrectly assumed I shared his religious priorities. During my presentation I sensed the chaplain was uneasy with my words. Afterward, he said he likely wouldn't invite me to return, that most of the inmates lacked the capacity to reason and reflect and were better served by a more structured worldview. While I think he was overgeneralizing, I do think he might have been right about the inability of some people to deal with nuance and ambiguity. I find those traits liberating and helpful, but it is clear others prefer lists, codes, rules, and boundaries. Those people likely won't expand our understanding of God and ourselves, they tend not to be spiritual pioneers, but if narrow and codified religion keeps them from harming themselves or others, then such a religion can be useful. I wouldn't choose it for myself, but I'm grateful it works for them.

A religion centered on holiness codes has never appealed to me, but I know others have found such an approach to God meaningful, helping them order their world around clear rules of lifestyle, dress, and conduct. Sometimes, I have been dismissive of those who approach God through set-in-stone rules. Some who value a more concrete faith leave no room for a more mystical or open approach to God. Our mutual failure was our lack of imagination—our assumption that just because we didn't find something personally helpful it would therefore be unhelpful to all. It might well be the height of spiritual maturity to look closely at another's religion and say, "I would not choose that faith for myself, but I am grateful it works for them." And believing that, resisting the temptation to make them like ourselves.

Why It Matters

While the persons I cited were more traditional believers, progressive people of faith have their own holiness codes, their own standards they embrace, believing they capture the essence of God and therefore must be heeded. Several years ago, I gave a speech supporting the full rights of trans people, but I was condemned by several persons afterward when I published the speech for using the word *transgendered instead of transgender.* That word, they argued, implied something had been done to trans people. While I wasn't searching for compliments, I did think it interesting that none of those who reprimanded me expressed appreciation for my defense of a marginalized group. I had violated the language code, which apparently nullified my concern for justice. But then, this is what holiness codes do—they demand obedience to the particulars, often at the expense of the larger goal.

I understand the appeal of holiness codes, but there are dangers in thinking God despises the same things we do. First, such thinking lends divine authority to our prejudices. Before the Nazis in Germany exterminated the first Jew, they had to convince themselves God hated the Jewish people as much as they did. They did this so thoroughly, so convincingly, they believed hating Jews was their religious duty, something God required of them. They could, and did, proclaim *Gott Mit Uns* or "God with Us," giving themselves tacit permission to do whatever they wished.

If you tend to be traditional, and are uncomfortable with interracial marriage, homosexuality, women in leadership, socialism, trans people, or any other thing or person different from you, that doesn't mean God is. Likewise, if you are socially progressive and consequently hold certain beliefs and attitudes, that doesn't necessarily mean God shares your passions. *God does not exist to confirm our preferences.* Indeed, if we notice God always seems to like the same things we do, it probably means we've been worshipping an idol, in this instance our own inclinations. It must never be forgotten that God is always more than we are.

Chapter 7

Regarding Sex

When I was a kid, a group of folks, unhappy with their church and in search of more excitement, started a new church and had the bright idea to hire a young person to be their youth pastor. Up until then, Jerry Sipes's parents had headed up the youth group, meeting with the kids on Sunday evenings to talk with them about things they should avoid, chief among them sex. I attended one of the meetings, hoping it might be a tutorial, and was amazed someone could talk about reproduction for an entire hour without ever mentioning specific body parts. A short time later, the new church hired a college kid who played the guitar and sang songs about Jesus, then concluded the evening with a talk about venereal diseases and their effects on various appendages. The college kid was handsome, and my female classmates flocked to the youth group, taking vows of chastity just as my interest in them was

beginning to peak. It was as if my town's entire religious population were committed to my celibacy.

Because the church shirked its obligation to teach me about
such matters, I had to glean whatever information I could from
upperclassmen and, when they were unavailable, to scour *The
Police Gazette* at the Danville Rexall when Thad Cramer, the
pharmacist, wasn't watching. As a consequence I was embar-
rassingly misinformed about sexual matters and for years believed babies were conceived by playing poker, until I was in
high school and Bill Eddy told me they were made by dancing.
Fortunately, I hadn't done either one and remained childless
well into my thirties, when my wife and I attended a wedding
and danced. Nine months later, our first child was born. A few
years after that, we danced again and our second son came
along.

It's different today, of course, now that kids can go online
and learn all kinds of things their churches and parents don't
want them to know. I'm of two minds about this. Though generally in favor of knowledge and the wide dissemination of
useful information, I also believe in the beauty of childhood
innocence and hate to see it end just as soon as kids are able to
Google words they heard on television shows their Christian
parents were watching when they thought their children were
asleep.

We've created a society in which commercial interests rep-
resenting distorted and unhealthy views on sexuality are the
first to inform our children about it. I'm not sure whose fault
this is, but I suspect the church bears some of the blame, having told us sex shouldn't be discussed in public or taught in

schools. When emotionally healthy folks refuse to acknowledge and discuss sexuality, the unhealthy will.

Regarding sex, I was doubly cursed, growing up in the Catholic Church, which appeared so fearful of sexual intimacy they didn't permit their leaders to experience it. Of course, when sexuality isn't allowed to express itself in a lovely and gracious manner, it will often express itself in a sordid, manipulative way. When the molestation of children by priests became known, I was as shocked as anyone, until I began to think how systems of oppression and denial, coupled with a lack of accountability, often create patterns of abuse and evil. Sadly, abusive clergy aren't confined to the Catholic Church but can be found in any institution where a handful of immature people are granted inordinate power, permitting distorted understandings of intimacy to prevail. And doesn't it seem like the pastors and priests who rail most frequently against sexual sin are often the ones committing it?

As I said, I was doubly cursed. Raised in a Catholic culture of sexual repression, then enticed into the evangelical camp, who matched the Catholics item for item on things to feel guilty about, first and foremost any stray thoughts I might have entertained about the opposite sex. I joined the evangelicals following my happy discovery that the girls in that fold were prettier than the Catholic girls I knew, though all of them seemed willing, almost cheerfully so, to live their lives without me.

About this time, our neighbors across the street moved away and a new family moved in, a family so indifferent about Christianity we could only surmise they were going to hell, which I pointed out to them, but they seemed indifferent about that, too. I was intrigued by their apathy, having never met an entire family so impervious to religion. A few weeks later, I witnessed firsthand the extent of their depravity while seated on their front porch with one of their sons. The mailman came up their sidewalk pushing his cart, stepped onto their porch, and handed the son that day's mail.

"Oh, look," the son said, thumbing through the mail, "Dad's *Playboy* came today."

He began leafing through the magazine, perusing Miss July. At least I think he did. I had fainted dead away, certain God was going to strike us down. When I recovered, he was studying the centerfold, then asked if I wanted it. I was fourteen, and a boiling cauldron of hormones, so of course I wanted it. I grabbed it before he changed his mind, ran home, and hid it under my mattress. That night, I fell asleep while reading it, and when my mother entered my bedroom to make sure her Christian son was tucked in for the night, there I lay, asleep, the centerfold draped across me.

My mother was a school principal, and not much rattled her. She handled the situation like she did most things, with a cuff upside the head and a lecture, both of which she delivered at the breakfast table the next morning, before launching into a long-overdue talk on the birds and the bees, which I had no need of, having read all about them in *Playboy* the day before. I didn't point that out, but instead sat quietly and listened, and when she wanted to know if I had any questions, asked if it were true what the nuns had told us, that boys who touched their wieners went blind.

"Yes," my mother said to her only son who wore eyeglasses, "it's true."

This is how I grew up, surrounded by adults who seemed curiously uninformed about the one human activity that ensures the continuity of our species. When my sons were entering their teen years, I took great pains to teach them that self-enjoyment doesn't lead to blindness, but has been known to cause horrible acne.

The church's reluctance to discuss human sexuality has resulted in its knee-jerk tendency to see sin wherever sex is involved. The list starts with masturbation, winds its way through teenage touching and premarital sex, then takes a swing at gays and lesbians before rounding on trans persons, as if our sexual natures were shameful and unnatural, invented by Satan, instead of God's nifty little way of making up for suffering and loneliness.

It wasn't always this way. When the author of the Song of Solomon wrote about divine love, the closest parallel he could find was human intimacy. But let a pastor stand in the pulpit today and read from the Song of Solomon and she'll be looking for a new job, fired by the very folks who rush to declare that all the Bible, every last jot and tittle, is holy and true.

I once pastored a church in which a man and woman in the congregation, well into their eighties, had lost their spouses, then were fortunate enough to meet each other and share companionship. Two of their adult children accused them of disrespecting their deceased spouses by dating again. The couple feared marriage might cause an irreparable rift in their respective families, so decided against it. They did, however, share meals and spend the occasional night together. At the time, our nation was involved in a war in the Persian Gulf, an action enthusiastically supported by several folks in the church, who reminded us each week to pray for the complete and utter annihilation of Iraqi fathers and sons, most of whom had been forced into military service. Blind to that evil, they saved their moral indignation for two aging congregants falling asleep in each other's arms.

Our preoccupation with sex has caused some in the church to lose all sense of reality and proportion. When the Twin Towers were knocked down by terrorists, it took roughly five seconds for Jerry Falwell and Pat Robertson to blame the whole mess on gay people, which, unless those nineteen hijackers were all gay, seems a bit of a stretch. Since then, I have seen gay people blamed for the decline in church attendance, the Ebola breakout in Africa, the election of President Obama, China's rising dominance, a weakened U.S. military, and the Zika virus. If all that is true, it's a wonder gay people find time to sleep.

However, something interesting is happening. As our understanding of sexual diversity deepens, more people are sympathetic to the challenges faced by sexual minorities, and more are likely to support efforts toward full inclusion. Younger people, even some who belong to evangelical churches, don't share their elders' biases against gays and lesbians. When the Supreme Court affirmed the right of marriage for homosexuals, it became clear the hateful rhetoric against them would no longer be tolerated by the upcoming generation. Indeed, the fastest way to lose young people in any church is for that church's pastor to attack gays and lesbians from the pulpit.

Having been deprived of that target, some in the church set their sights on trans people, making their lives a fresh hell by calling for laws restricting their use of restrooms. I was staggered, that is the only word that suffices, by how quickly this issue rose to national prominence. It was as if trans people had suddenly laid siege to restrooms nationwide, preying on women and children, though I hadn't heard any instances of that happening, nor had anyone else, for that matter. It was enough to suggest the possibility of such a threat to roil our cultural waters.

Lacking in the discourse was any effort to truly understand why some people, roughly one third of one percent of the population, are transgender. Given the complexities of gender and sexual formation, it's amazing our gender and sexual patterns aren't more varied than they are. Because of the relative rarity of trans people, one would hope we could be sympathetic to the emotional struggles sexual minorities have faced in their self-understanding, and commit ourselves to their well-being. Instead, we have demonized them, punishing them for characteristics they neither chose nor sought. It would be no different from waking up one morning determined to condemn people with red hair.

I wonder how different our national conversation might have been if churches had taken a more enlightened approach to sexuality. Sadly, the church's fear of sex has, in some quarters, prohibited a thoughtful examination of human development, leading to a reactionary and narrow response to sexual differences. This fear has been coupled with a tendency toward unreality. Rather than acknowledging the biological urges of young people and discussing appropriate expressions of human sexuality, we dismissed those desires as sinful, making it nearly impossible for young people to seek helpful counsel. Instead of studying the causes of homosexuality, we rejected that orientation as immoral, making it doubly difficult for young people to better understand themselves and others.

On one occasion, years ago, a young woman and her mother came to my office. I didn't know them; they were distantly related to members of the Quaker meeting I was pastoring at the time. The mother and daughter had been at odds and were, to their credit, wanting to discuss their differences with a neutral third party, who turned out to be me. I asked each of them if she had anything to say to the other, something she had been holding back. The daughter said she did, then turned to her mother and told her she had never been attracted to men.

The mother, sensing where the conversation was headed, covered her ears and said, "Don't say it, don't say it, don't say it!"

She was incapable of discussing her daughter's sexuality. But more than incapable, she believed her daughter's sexual orientation wouldn't "take" as long as it remained unacknowledged. It also became clear her views were motivated by her religious beliefs, which were deeply entrenched and not likely to change. Sadly, they haven't yet. And though the mother and daughter are cordial with each other, the warmth they once enjoyed has cooled.

This might be one of the more troubling aspects of religious beliefs, their doggedness and durability. Since changing our minds on religious matters is often viewed as being unfaithful, we are more likely to persist in our beliefs, even as they harm our relationships. When our understanding of human sexuality is negatively informed by our religious faith, we are unlikely to engage in the kind of discourse necessary for growth. We become set in our ways, resistant to scientific evidence, resentful when the currents of time, culture, and science sweep away views we once thought unassailable. It's no wonder so many people seeking elective office promise to return us to yesterday's fabled morality. That promise is almost guaranteed to win them a passionate following of people who long for a time we will never know again, and in fact never have known.

When I was in junior high, I found myself fantasizing about my female classmates. At the time, I didn't realize my thoughts and feelings were common for young people in the throes of puberty. Having been taught by the church that sexual thoughts are sinful, I was too ashamed to discuss my yearnings with the adults in my life. And none of them were lining up to discuss these matters with me, at least until my mother caught me with a *Playboy*.

At the end of my seventh-grade year, our phys ed teacher spent a week teaching the boys the differences between boys and girls. It was a dry recitation of biological facts, with no effort to explain the many dimensions of human intimacy. It reduced sex to a mechanical, physical act, devoid of joy, awareness, and love. Perhaps we would have been incapable of understanding such things in the seventh grade, but it would have been nice to have had them explained. Nor was there, that I can remember, any assurance that sexual thoughts and feelings are normal and important parts of our physical and emotional growth. I don't fault our teacher. He was working from a pamphlet that could have been written by a plumber for its detached, mechanical approach. What stays with me is the memory of sex reduced to a physical act, stripped of its warmth, love, and spirit.

This was also the case on the few occasions the church talked about sex. There was no recognition of the beauty and wonder of human intimacy, just cold, stark warnings of its dangers. The church had succeeded in taking one of the most transcendent moments of human experience and reducing it to a perilous, sordid act. The irony wasn't lost on me that the priests and nuns warning us about sexual intimacy had likely never experienced it themselves. It was like someone who had never flown trying to explain the wondrous miracle of soaring above the clouds.

The church's failure to speak intelligently and realistically about human intimacy, sexual orientation, and gender formation has created a void in our cultural conversation, encouraging the least mature among us to fill that vacuum with a demeaning, degrading view of sex. When sex is too easily and quickly dismissed as sin, its practice will become distorted and destructive. Until it is acknowledged as a gift from God, it will remain the domain of Hollywood and the Kardashians, who, I assure you, don't seem all that committed to our happiness and growth.

Why It Matters

Human intimacy is sacramental, an outward sign of an inward reality—the mutuality of divine and human love. In it, we give of ourselves to another, and receive the other's gift to us. It is delightful, life-affirming, a celebration of our affection, even our adoration, of our beloved. Outside of this context, it reminds us of love's absence, of what we want desperately to have but do not. Sexual pleasure with the person we love reminds us that God wants us to enjoy life, that our bodies were created not only for work but for joy and pleasure.

I have a friend who was making love to his wife and glanced up to see their five-year-old son, whom they had thought was in bed, taking in their activity. My friend was chuckling when he mentioned it to me.

"That would be horrible," I said. "I hope that never happens to me."

"I don't think my child will be scarred by accidentally seeing his parents make love," he said. "What if we had been fighting or yelling at one another? Would that have been better?"

Of course he was right. What does it say about us when our intimacy is an embarrassment and our hostility is normalized? How often have we told our children, when they have caught us arguing, "All parents fight. It doesn't mean anything." Of course it means something. It means we have forsaken our vows, if only for a moment, to love and cherish each other.

Healthy religion embraces intimacy and affection. It appreciates how the tenderness between people represents, in a very real way, God's love for humankind. In light of that, sex is a holy act, a moment in which we transcend ourselves to participate in something indescribably sacred. It would be a good sign of our spiritual well-being if, when asked to describe a moment we felt close to God, we said, "When I loved another."

Chapter 8

God Is Everywhere,
but Mostly in America

It was a neighbor, Mrs. Vaughn, who first told me God is an American, having taken up residence when Christopher Columbus arrived in our neck of the woods in 1492, before we were even a country. I was still a kid when informed of God's citizenship and hadn't given God a lot of thought, but I do remember the nuns saying that God is everywhere, so I was a bit mystified that God wasn't standing on the shores welcoming Columbus when he arrived. But Mrs. Vaughn seemed confident about the matter. She said Columbus brought God to America with him in order to convert the heathen savages. Unfortunately, he also brought them smallpox, but at least they knew God and went to heaven when they died in an agony of fever and sores.

It was the consensus among the Christians in our town that God and America were thick as thieves. There was an American flag in the Catholic church I attended, and one in the Protestant church where I went to play basketball on Saturday mornings. One day, while riding my bicycle past the Baptist church, I noticed its door standing open, so I entered and saw an American flag in there, too—a ginormous one, stretched across the front of the sanctuary. In my memory it was hot, so it must have been near the Fourth of July.

When I began attending the Quaker meeting as a teenager, I was pleased to see they had an American flag. At least people wouldn't think I was unpatriotic like they did my friend Joe, who attended the Jehovah's Witness Kingdom Hall south of our town in the country. When I asked him if there were a flag in their church, he told me there wasn't, then told me I wasn't going to enjoy paradise on earth since my church had a flag. Joe had clear opinions about God, few of which I shared even then.

A teenager down the street was drafted and sent to Vietnam. When I asked why, I was told we were fighting godless communism and God needed our help. I wondered why God couldn't fight the communists by himself since he was all-powerful, and was told it was our job to bring God to the people of Vietnam. Killing them seemed an odd way to do that, but what did I know? I was just a kid, and it was a confusing time. What did seem clear was that so many Americans believed Christianity wasn't just about following Jesus. It was also about being a good American, voting for Richard Nixon, flying the flag, and pledging our allegiance each morning at school. One nation, under God. The two were inseparable, joined at the hip. To love one was to love the other.

For many years, well into adulthood, I thought believing

in God was our duty as Americans. I was pretty certain it said that in the Constitution, and if it didn't, it was merely an oversight by our nation's founders and should be remedied with a new amendment. Occasionally, I would meet an atheist and wonder how someone could be American and not believe in God. Couldn't they see the hand of God in the founding and formation of our nation? Didn't they appreciate the godly endeavors our nation had undertaken to better the world? How could they not value America's unique role as God's agent in the world, and be grateful for the blessings God had conferred upon our nation?

Naturally, if the hand of God was upon America, it stood to reason that God directed our nation, and it was therefore up to each of us to cooperate with God's plan. But how could we know that plan? Easy. Whatever America did was God's plan. If we went to war, it was because God willed it. If some were rich and others were poor, it was God's will, and not the consequence of economic systems that rewarded some and penalized others. Therefore, if the economic system failed us, it was our personal fault, and not an indication of systemic imbalance, since God had ordained our capitalist system. Later, when I read Jesus's comments about the rich, I began to wonder if God were as enamored with capitalism as I had been taught.

God-infused nationalism can be sustained only if no one questions it, which is why we have always treated skeptics and doubters so harshly. In questioning this holy alliance, they tug at the thread that might cause the whole tapestry to unravel. One such doubter, in my home state of Indiana, was a man named Eugene Debs, who was placed on trial in 1918 for violating the Sedition Act, a treacherous little piece of legislation that allowed the authorities to imprison anyone for the crime of thinking differently. At Debs's trial, he said to the judge, "I am opposing a social order in which it is possible for one man who does absolutely nothing that is useful to amass a fortune of hundreds of millions of dollars, while millions of men and women who work all the days of their lives secure barely enough for a wretched existence." The judge was not impressed and sentenced Debs to prison. We've always had a knack for silencing or sidelining those who've opposed our divinely mandated structures and priorities.

In the buildup to our invasion of Iraq, I was speaking at a conference when a man stood during the question-and-answer period and criticized President George W. Bush's decision to engage in war against a nation that hadn't attacked us. Afterward, three people quietly informed me the man was mentally ill. Their inference was obvious—one would have to be crazy to question American policy. I knew the man, had known him for years, and in all that time I had never witnessed in him any evidence of mental illness, but when I remarked that he seemed fine to me, these people looked at me as if I were insane. For this union of God and country to be sustained, those who question it must be seen as traitorous or mentally unhinged.

To be fair, the alliance of God and country wasn't an American invention, though we have raised it to an art form. But before us, European nations, with their invented divine mandate to colonize and rule the world, ingeniously linked God's favor to national well-being. No expedition in search of new lands went forth without a cleric on board, conferring God's blessing on their nation's endeavors. Isn't it interesting that whenever these nations sent soldiers to war, they included, and still include, clergy in their ranks? Though these clerics provide emotional support to the armed forces, they also, by their very presence, imply God's partnership in war.

Long before Europeans and Americans joined God and country, the nation of Israel married the two. And not just the Israelites but many ancient nation-states and tribes laid claim to gods whose favor always seemed to settle most abundantly upon them. It became a simple matter, when we read the accounts of those nations, especially the stories enshrined in Scripture, to adopt their language and philosophy as our own. So America became a chosen nation, blessed and favored by God, just as Israel claimed to be. We interpreted our history in light of that chosen status, taught that history to our children and grandchildren until the myth of divine favor was part and parcel of our nation's story.

The church supported this claim, since its alliance with America's story added to its own luster and power. When America's courts and leaders failed to endorse the church's priorities, the church often responded by threatening the retraction of God's blessing. "God will bless America when America blesses God!" That stale and dubious proclamation was uttered most often when someone dared suggest gay people should have the same rights as everyone else, or women should control their reproductive choices. Conversely, when the government affirmed the church's power, the church assured the nation of God's favor, as if it actually had the power to do so. It didn't take much to satisfy the church—the addition of the words "under God" to the pledge of allegiance in 1954, and "In God We Trust" to paper currency in 1957. The church then promised all sorts of divine blessing in the decades ahead, but instead we got persistent segregation, the Vietnam War, Richard Nixon, and the leisure suit.

But worse than that, as if there could be anything worse than leisure suits, the interests of God and country became so closely aligned we soon made no distinction between the two. The values of the nation became the values of God. So when our nation went to war, God blessed that war and became a warrior. When our nation developed an elite and wealthy class, a few that ruled the many, God became the god of the oligarchs, preserving the power of the few and sanctifying the process that let them rise. Indeed, we are in just such a period now, aided and abetted not only by the oligarchs but by the evangelicals who put them in power. Should we descend into angry, hateful factions, God is likely to become angry and hateful. God will become whatever the nation values. No higher, no better, no purer.

Our efforts to unite God and country, to pretend as if their objectives and characters are one, is to create a tribal god, who cares only for its own and no one else. It is the god of limited love, who endorses massacres, holocausts, and injustice of every sort, so long as those tyrannies are directed against the other. This sad union is the parent of war, terrorism, and hypernationalism, giving birth to unbridled evil if not checked by the rule of law.

I see other losses. When God and country are joined at the hip, the capacity to critique the nation is stopped, for it is one thing to question or criticize a country, a politician, or a party but another thing altogether to question or criticize God.

I once attended a worship service with an acquaintance who had been inviting me to visit his church for several years. When I realized it would be easier to attend than to make excuses every month for the rest of my life, I took a Sunday off from my Quaker meeting and went to his church. I wasn't sure what he expected from me. I wasn't going to toss aside my own community to join his, but he had recently done a favor for me, so I reasoned that spending a Sunday morning with him would be the kind thing to do, and relatively painless. I was, of course, mistaken. It was a positively dreadful experience from which I've still not recovered.

The pastor repeatedly declared, as he was manhandling several Bible verses, that if the congregation didn't agree with him, they should take it up with God, whose words he was speaking. I feel perfectly comfortable dismissing that sort of spiritual manipulation, recognizing it as the fallback position of pastors who can't tolerate dissent or critique. But I noticed others in the room nodding their heads in agreement. In their minds, to disagree with their pastor was to disagree with God.

Just as some are unable to separate the demands of their pastors from the demands of God, some are unable to make any distinction between the claims of God and those of country. To serve one is to serve the other. To honor one is to honor the other. Conversely, to doubt one is to doubt the other. This, as you can imagine, has a chilling effect on the church's ability to speak prophetically when the government acts unethically, which, being a human creation, it regularly does.

Can we trust the church to critique any government it believes embodies the will and purpose of God?

This is why Christians, in their journey toward faithfulness, must draw a sharp distinction between the priorities of God and the concerns of country. While those values might at times overlap, especially in those moments when a nation seeks to alleviate human suffering through peaceful means, at other times their values will be at cross-purposes. We mustn't forget that the chief, though unspoken, aim of almost every government is the attainment of wealth and the consolidation of power. Those were hardly the priorities of Jesus. No amount of flag waving and public prayer can reconcile the two philosophies. Printing religious sentiments on our currency in no way purifies our nation's economic practices. The worship of mammon continues unabated no matter what religious slogans we print upon our currency.

We can be deeply appreciative of and grateful for our country, but we mustn't let our pride blind us to the virtues and qualities of other nations. Wouldn't America be better served if its citizens enjoyed universal health care like those of every other industrialized nation in the world? Wouldn't we be fortunate to have the 100 percent literacy rate of Finland and five other nations? Wouldn't we be blessed to have Taiwan's 1.5 percent poverty rate? Or Monaco's 89 years of life expectancy? Or Iceland's virtually nonexistent murder rate? Unfortunately, our insistence that America is uniquely blessed by God, which implies a sort of holy perfection, blinds us to the many challenges we face. Surely it is possible to be grateful for the many advantages we enjoy, whether those advantages are the results of divine benevolence or accidents of history and geography, but still acknowledge that our experiment in democracy requires ongoing refinement.

Several years ago, I was invited to speak at a conference on religious life in America. I didn't realize when agreeing to speak that I would be expected to defend the doctrine of America as God's chosen nation, so I spoke instead about the inherent dangers of religious overreach in a democracy. My speech was received about as well as you might imagine. During the question-and-answer session that followed my presentation, I was accused not only of historical ignorance but of heresy. This illustrates the near reverence in which the cultural marriage of God and country is held. To hold a contrary view of our nation's divine stature is not just contrary but sinful!

On another occasion, in the winter of 2003, I was speaking at a church and asked by the person leading worship to close the service with a prayer for our military success in Iraq, a nation we were preparing to invade. Instead I prayed we would resolve our disagreements peacefully. I also acknowledged God's love for the people of Iraq. Several persons thanked me afterward, though many more left without speaking to me. It is possible to pray for military success only when we're persuaded God sides with us. While that was an easier argument to make in World War II because of Hitler's horrific atrocities, today's pattern of endless war casts doubt on divine endorsements.

We must find a way to be simultaneously people of faith

and citizens of America without acting as if the two are one. By their very natures, they demand separate things from us. Occasionally, their priorities overlap, but not nearly as often as we imagine. When their priorities collide, we must discern which community we will serve. That decision is ours to make, of course, but we must not delude ourselves in thinking that to serve one is to serve the other.

Why It Matters

What does the marriage of faith and nationalism say about God, and how does it affect our world? How does our failure to delineate between divine and national priorities shape our worldview and faith? Doesn't it have a tendency to "shrink" God, reducing God to a regional player, with little concern for the wider world? How can we speak of a God who created the universe while simultaneously believing God is uniquely devoted to a microscopic slice of that universe? It would be no different than extolling the love of a mother for her children even as that mother sought to bless only one of them.

Until nations transcend their regional gods, there will never be peace. Until religions refuse to be exploited by those seeking divine endorsement for their political gain, the priorities of God will never be achieved. Nation will be pitted against nation, faith against faith, even family against family, for the divisions that poison one nation against another seep outward, infecting us all. The antidote is our steadfast refusal to limit God's love to our own kind, and to embrace instead the universal aspect of God that permeates all creation.

Consider this: The true saints of the church aren't those

with an impassioned zeal for God and country but those whose vision of the Divine inspires them to see all people as fellow citizens of God's wide Reign. It is as concerned for the Syrian child washed up on Turkey's shore as it is for its own. Having no enemies except hate itself, it sees the Light of God in all, even if that Light is only a flickering spark.

I had the pleasure of knowing just such a saint, a woman named Fern Reed Hadley. I met her as I was entering this world of wider faith and she was departing it. An elderly Quaker, she labored diligently and cheerfully as one of God's emissaries. It was a joy to know her, and to be known by her. Well into her eighties, she died suddenly while traveling through Portugal. Her body was donated to a medical school in that nation, and a memorial service was held several weeks later at the Quaker meeting we both attended. During the service, a family member traveling with her and present at her death had this to say: "We had no sooner arrived at our hotel room when Fern set about making it feel like home. She did that wherever we went, so that within an hour you felt as if you had lived there all your life. You felt as if you had come home."

It is this "at-homeness" the true saints create wherever they reside. They feel at home in all the world, just as God is at home in all the world, and not just some privileged corner. Because all the world is home to them, all people are their neighbors. They have no fear of the stranger, no suspicion of the different. They welcome all, care for all, seek the best for all. They do not believe divine chosenness is linked to one's citizenship, so do not claim a blessing for themselves they would then deny to others.

When Jesus said, "Foxes have dens and birds have nests,

but the Son of Man has no place to lay his head," perhaps it was a statement not of his poverty but of his at-homeness in the world. To own no specific place in which to lay your head is to be not bound by geography, and consequently to be free to lay your head wherever you choose, with whomever you wish, no matter their nation or tribe. We saw this freedom revealed when Jesus laid his head at the home of Zacchaeus, when he lingered to pray at Gethsemane, when he stayed the night in Bethany. Because no one place was his home, everywhere had the potential to be.

You and I are called to a life that transcends borders and boundaries, since no human construct can capture or contain the wide embrace of God. God flies no flag but the banner of love, under which we all reside.

Chapter 9

God Is a Trespasser

When I was in high school, the worst thing that could ever happen to a teenager happened to me. My mother, along with a few other mothers at St. Mary's Queen of Peace Catholic Church, decided to do something about the steady migration of the church's youth over to the Protestants by beginning a youth group that would meet at our house on Sunday evenings. Since I'd recently been caught with a *Playboy* magazine, the mothers decided they would talk to the church's teenagers about sex, the prospect of which filled us with dread and caused us to consider mass suicide. An unusually high percentage of the students in the youth group later announced they were homosexual, leading me to believe for several years that homosexuality was caused by acute embarrassment during puberty.

The mothers didn't jump headlong into the topic of sex.

Instead, they began talking to us about marriage, referring to it as a sacrament, an outward sign of an inward grace. They told us there are seven sacraments. First there was *baptism*, typically done during infancy so the recipients couldn't object. Then there was *confirmation*, which happened around the age of seven and was the church's way of reminding its children that just because they'd been baptized didn't mean they were home free. After confirmation came *communion*, taking Christ's body and blood into us, to make us more like Jesus, even though it felt slightly cannibalistic if you thought about it very long, so I didn't. Next came *confession* or *reconciliation*, where we told the priest what we'd been up to, sin-wise, and he then announced God's forgiveness and sent us out with a clean slate, which we promptly refilled with fresh new sins. Then *marriage* came along, for everyone except the priests and nuns, which likely explains why it's hard these days to find folks willing to be priests and nuns. This led to the next sacrament, *holy orders*, when priests and nuns vow to serve the church, proclaim the gospel, and generally make people feel guilty. The last sacrament is the *anointing of the sick*, a ritual of healing for the physically, mentally, and spiritually ill. The Catholics are most fuzzy about this one, since a lot of people undergoing the ritual don't get measurably better, but it's worth a try and certainly cheaper than a hospital stay.

So our mothers taught us about the sacraments, all seven of them, and said that when we participate in them we experience the presence of God. I'd spoken to enough people to know that was true, that participating in the sacraments did make them feel close to God. What I objected to, then and now, was their assertion that God can be known only through the sacraments. I enjoyed hiking in the woods, and on occasion while there even experienced great awe and wonder. When I mentioned that to our mothers, I was told walking in the woods isn't a sacrament. They warned me that my time in nature might take me away from God, causing me to worship trees or the sun, which would result in me, when I died, spending eternity apart from God, in eternal torment. So I stayed out of the woods for several years, and instead bought a car and went cruising for girls, knowing nothing bad could come of that.

Around that same time, a book on Native American spirituality was donated to our town's public library. It caused a ruckus among certain Christians, who wrote letters to the editor warning about paganism and how anyone who read the book would land in hell. So of course I read it and was shocked to discover that the Native Americans experienced the presence of God in numerous ways. They saw God in the sky and the lakes and rivers, in the animals and trees. They felt God's spirit blow upon them in the wind. They experienced God's providential care in the animals they hunted, the crops they grew, and the rains that bathed the land. In fact, these "uncivilized savages" seemed to possess a rather expansive view of God and creation that made our views seem destructively myopic in comparison.

But I remember being afraid while reading that book, scared I might be caught reading it, even more frightened about it than about being caught reading a *Playboy*. The *Playboy*, after all, could be explained away by adolescent curiosity. But being caught with a book that defied the church's teachings was a threat to my eternal soul, and something God wasn't likely to forgive. I could hear our mothers telling us God's presence is conveyed through the seven sacraments, and only through them, and only if administered by a Roman Catholic priest who had been ordained by a bishop in apostolic succession, as if there had been an unbroken chain of authority dating back to Peter, even in the thirty-nine years from 1378 to 1417, when three different men simultaneously claimed to be the pope. But other than that, God was careful to be present only in those seven sacraments, no more, no less. And don't let anyone tell you differently.

As you would expect, when I first learned of Native Americans' spirituality, I believed they were headed to hell. I thought the same thing when I went to the Baptist church with my sister and was told there are only two sacraments, baptism and communion, and not just any kind of baptism, but baptism by immersion—your entire body held underwater—which happened to my sister, who kicked and thrashed and came up looking like a drowned rat. The pastor said she was a new person, even though she appeared to be the same old sister to me, albeit damper.

I explained all of this to a Lutheran friend, who told me the Catholics and Baptists wouldn't know God if he kicked them in the shins, and said there are three sacraments—baptism, communion, and penance. Later, in a daring departure from my childhood faith and not without some fear, I began attending a Quaker meeting and was told by the pastor that Quakers don't believe in sacraments, which I believed for quite a while, until I realized he was mistaken. What he meant to say, but didn't know quite how to say, was that Quakers don't practice outward sacraments but emphasize instead the inward spiritual experience that the outward sacraments symbolize. But more than that, Quakers believe the reality of God can be known in an infinite number of ways, not just seven, or two, or three. Quakers aren't antisacramental but *pansacramental,* believing all of creation reveals God if only we cultivate our capacity to see the Divine Presence.

I was mildly excited just now when I used the word *pansacramental,* thinking I had made up a new word and that other people would use it and quote me and I'd be cited one day in dry theological tomes. But it turns out a theologian named Martin Buber coined the word and by it meant a mystical appreciation for all creation, animate and inanimate, which is what I'm getting at when I talk about the ability to see God in all of life, and not just in the seven, two, or three specified ways the church has claimed.

Haven't you also found this to be true? That God is present not only in the most obvious places—a hospital delivery room, a cathedral of forest trees, the seaside, a house of worship, places of great beauty—but also in the most unlikely times and places, when we least expect to encounter grace—in a moment of loss, in the midst of suffering and pain, when we're lonely and afraid, among the poverty-stricken? God is a trespasser, with no respect for boundaries. God butts in here, noses around there, and is just as likely to be found outside religion as inside it. Her essence and spirit is known as intimately by a high school dropout as by a Harvard theologian.

I eventually concluded God's presence is so expansive that

while God can be experienced in the sacraments, she is never confined to them. This implies, of course, that God is present beyond Christianity, its rituals, and its forms. When I began to say this publicly, I was denounced as a heretic. But ask people when God was most present to them, then sit back, listen, and learn.

A woman I know tells me the peace of God seemed most present to her not during her baptism, as her pastor had assured her would be the case, but in a hospital room decades later when her twenty-five-year-old daughter died of cancer.

An alcoholic I know has taken communion every Sunday morning at his church since the age of eight. While he finds that meaningful, he's told me several times he experiences the presence of God most vividly on Wednesday evenings when he attends AA, in what he calls the "fellowship of the broken." There, he finds honesty, forgiveness, belief, and faith, often to a degree he doesn't find in church.

For years, I believed God was nearest to me when I sat in silence with my fellow Quakers. While I continue to find that meaningful, I'm just as likely to feel engaged with God when star-watching, walking in the woods, or holding my grand-daughter. And there's a lovely riff, 6:47 minutes into Eric Clapton's "Layla," recorded at his 1999 concert at Madison Square Garden, that is as close to holy perfection as anything I've ever known. Is that a sacrament, too? Some in the church would say no, yet I feel transported when hearing it.

How odd that the one institution tasked with helping us see God in the world tends to number the ways in which she is known. Shouldn't the exact opposite be true? Shouldn't the church equip people to see and experience God in all of life? Why this marking of boundaries, this tendency to corral God, to say God is present in one place but not another, in some activities but not others? Throughout history, haven't the saints been those people who experienced the reality of God so broadly, yet so intimately, they made God seem alive and ever-present? And haven't the villains of history, before they've done anything else, first tried to convince others the presence and grace of God was limited to their kind, and their kind alone?

What if we simultaneously affirm the joy some have experienced in sacramental religion *and* acknowledge others have found that same Life in other persons, rituals, symbols, and experiences?

Why can't we treasure our own encounters with God without diminishing the encounters of others? Our willingness and ability to do just that may be key to our survival, since a good part of the world's hostility is rooted in religion, an indication of humanity's refusal to value one another's experience of God.

When I critique my childhood faith, I do not fault the ways my Catholic and evangelical peers experience God. I take them at their word that their holy encounters are real and meaningful for them. What I find troubling is our historic tendency to diminish the divine encounters of others. I was reminded on a weekly basis that I belonged to the One True Church, and others didn't, that the sacraments were an indication of God's preference for us, and others were lost.

When I became a Quaker, I met people who behaved as if

sacraments were the greatest threat to Christianity. I was sharing a meal one evening with the late Episcopalian writer and
scholar Marcus Borg, who asked me how Quakers in Indiana
were faring. I told him there was much division in our denomination because one of our Quaker meetings had begun
performing water baptisms. I must have sounded indignant
at this apostasy, because he good-naturedly gasped and said,
"Oh, my! What is the church coming to?"

In an instant, I saw his point—that with all the problems
in the world, why was a Quaker meeting's willingness to im-
merse those who wished to be baptized in water the cause of
such angst and anger among Friends? Why had that become
the proverbial line in the sand? Was our faith so meager it
could be damaged by another's decision to participate in an act
we wouldn't choose for ourselves?

Later that evening, I thought about the persons attending a Quaker meeting who hadn't grown up in our religious
tradition. Perhaps they had come to us from a tradition that
emphasized the necessity of water baptism. While Quakers
have historically emphasized the inward change of heart and
new birth as opposed to the outward ritual symbolizing that
change and birth, perhaps the new attendees were so afraid
of displeasing God, having previously been taught the ritual
was mandatory, that they asked the Quakers to depart from
custom so they could participate in the sacrament of baptism.
And let's suppose the Quaker meeting said no. Wouldn't it
then be true that the persons seeking baptism had been doubly
disserved by the church's intransigence? First, by the church
who had taught them the ritual of baptism was essential to a

proper relationship with God and second by a Quaker meeting who saw such little value in outward ceremonies it could not imagine why others might find them helpful.

It is this cold insistence to which I object, the church's failure to empathize with human struggles and fears. This is what must be unlearned. In nearly every instance, our fears arise from our conviction that we, and only we, have properly discerned the mind and will of God and therefore know what is best for others.

Shortly after that experience, I attended a Quaker meeting where I, along with others, was invited to pray for a member of the congregation who had joined the military and was serving in Afghanistan. That congregation dutifully supported one of its members away at war but was positively irate that another Quaker meeting had agreed to baptize a new member. I understand the desire to pray for the well-being of soldiers. My younger son serves as a medic in the Army, and I pray for him daily. But I do not understand our anger when religious protocols are violated, and our casual acceptance of war and violence. Is this what it means to be Christian in twenty-first-century America? Dotting our doctrinal *i*'s and crossing our sacramental *t*'s, straining at gnats, while the prophets of peace spin in their graves?

This reduction of spiritual matters to rote ritual leads inevitably to skewed priorities. The insight gained by our initial encounter with the Holy fades in importance as our devotion to sacramental and doctrinal purity increases. If communion was first intended to help us remember our participation in Christ's life, it soon became a gated entry into fellowship with

Jesus. The right words, the correct officiant, the proper setting became more important than the divine fellowship it sought to re-create and affirm. Some, the Quakers for instance, have responded to this tendency by rejecting outward sacraments. I'm not entirely sure that was a healthy response. Perhaps another option exists—a commitment to Martin Buber's *pansacramentalism,* cultivating our capacity to experience God everywhere in everything so that every moment is wonder-filled and, in its own way, holy.

Why It Matters

Why might a mystical appreciation for all creation, animate and inanimate, be so important? Here's what I've come to understand: Just as nationalism separates us from others, so does our insistence on sacramental superiority. Instead of elevating our place of birth, we exalt our orthodoxy, ultimately diminishing the spiritual experiences of others. It is akin to the Samaritan woman at the well, who said to Jesus, "Our ancestors worshipped on this mountain, but you Jews claim that the place where we must worship is in Jerusalem." It was then, and is now, an effort to distract others from meeting and knowing God, ourselves, and others. I suspect that as long as we can point out the shortcomings of others and emphasize our differences, we do not have to face our own limitations.

I have noticed my own tendency to dismiss the spiritual experiences of others, and have had to tamp down that temptation when writing this book. We must find a way to value our own insights without simultaneously diminishing the perspectives of others. To appreciate the path we have chosen doesn't require us to be antagonistic toward the paths of others. Neither does it mean we must surrender the richness of our personal experience. It simply means we must learn to appreciate the myriad ways people encounter the Divine Presence.

Until that day, life with God, and the joy it portends, has little chance of being realized on Earth, as it is in heaven.

Chapter 10

God Has a Plan for My Life

Ever since I was a kid I was taught God has a plan for my life. The people who told me that weren't talking to me specifically. I was one of a zillion Catholic kids crammed into a classroom, preparing for our first communion, which apparently was part of God's plan, something God knew I was going to do even before I was born. God knew who my parents would be, knew I'd have three brothers, one sister, and a dog named Zipper. Knew I wouldn't like vegetables, pineapple, or Jerry Sipes. Knew I was destined to be Catholic and go to heaven when I died. Knew when, where, and how I would die, though for some reason God had not seen fit to share the details with me.

God has a plan for all our lives, the nuns said.

"If someone isn't in the Catholic Church and they die and go to hell, was that God's plan?" Michael O'Brian asked.

Sister Peter Marie assured him it was.

"That doesn't seem fair," Michael said.

"It's not for us to decide what's fair and what isn't," she said. "That's God's business." Clearly, matters of existential justice were best left to God. Our job was simply to be grateful we weren't living in some squalid dung heap among the savages, never knowing about Jesus and the One True Church.

The nuns never revealed much detail about God's plan for my life, just that it would involve serving God by getting married and having lots of babies. A family in our church had six dozen kids and were so poor the girls bobby-pinned Kleenex to their heads instead of veils when they went forward for communion. Still, there was no doubt in our minds they were the best Catholics for miles around and would grow up to produce even more Catholics, all of them fertile, per God's plan.

Wanting more particulars than the nuns could provide, I asked my parents what God's plan for my life might be.

"You should maybe try sales," my salesman father said.

The idea was not without appeal. I sat in school and dreamed of visiting one small Indiana town after another, stopping at grocery and hardware stores, selling bug spray just like my father, eradicating mosquitoes, wasps, flies, and hornets. Or so I thought, until my mother suggested God's plan for me was to become a lawyer. By then, though, I was delivering newspapers and had three lawyers for customers, all of whom advised against it.

When I became a Quaker, the pastor had apparently been talking with the nuns, since he told me the exact same thing: God had a plan for my life, a very specific plan, right down to who I would marry, where I would work, and when I would die. It was my job, he said, to find out what that plan was and follow it. I wondered why God didn't tell me the plan and save us both a lot of trouble. Because what if I got it wrong? What if I spent years and years trying to figure out God's plan for my life and screwed everything up by becoming a brain surgeon when God had actually planned for me to become a wino? What if when I died after saving thousands of lives, God said, "You were supposed to be a wino so I could use you as a bad example. Instead, you disobeyed me and became a brain surgeon, so I'm sending you to hell."

To be on the safe side, I didn't enroll in college when I graduated from high school, not wanting to invest time and money in a vocation God might not want me to pursue. After five years, I told my pastor I wanted to be a pastor, which he thought was a fine idea, being one himself, so I quit my job and went to college and seminary and became a pastor. But sometimes I think maybe I should have been an architect and designed lovely houses for the poor, many of whom live in squalor and could use a little beauty in their lives. Wouldn't that please God?

I know enough pastors to suspect that when some of them announced that God had told them to become pastors, God likely thought, No, I didn't. I wanted you to stay twenty miles away from a pulpit. But they became pastors anyway and proceeded to tell people dumb things like God had a plan for their lives.

When I was dating, my pastor told me God had someone for everyone, not generally and theoretically, but specifically, a woman created just for me, and I for her.

"How will I know when I find her?" I asked him.

"You'll know," he promised.

A few years later I met my future wife and introduced her to my pastor, who told me he wasn't sure she was the one God had in mind for me. I married her anyway and we've been together over thirty-four years, though I know we're just kidding ourselves and the whole thing will blow up in our faces any day now. Then we'll each be free to find the one person we were intended to be with. I'm not sure how our children and grandchildren will feel about this, but who are they to argue with God's will?

Ironically, the same people who told me God had a specific plan for my life also told me God had given me a free will, which I should exercise to do God's will or be miserable. Isn't that a bit like the dictator who says, "You're free to vote for me, or free to go to jail. It's your choice." But how could we have it both ways? If God does have a specific plan for our lives, and if not following that plan makes us miserable, then few would consider themselves free.

When I still believed God had a specific plan for my life, I sometimes made myself sick worrying whether or not I would discover it, convinced if I didn't, I would be unhappy and lost. When I spoke with my spiritual guides, they assured me that if I prayed about it, God's will would become clear. So I prayed at some length but received no sign from God about what I should do. No opening the Bible to just the right verse, no dream about Jesus offering advice, no angel appearing and whispering in my ear. Then an elderly Quaker woman told me I should be a pastor, and even though she kind of annoyed me,

I decided to give it a try, believing God could hardly object to that. Still, when other pastors spoke convincingly about being called to ministry, I wondered why I hadn't felt such certainty.

Over the years, I've enjoyed my work immensely, yet I've learned that I could have happily done any number of things, none of which would have been wrong or bad. I've often wondered if the pastors' description of their work as a call from God is a not-so-subtle way of elevating their status. Why aren't other vocations seen as callings? The absence of the men who pick up trash in my town would be felt more sharply than mine. But why is my vocation deemed worthy of a calling from God and theirs is not?

I remember when my wife and I were first married and I said, "I don't know what I would have done if you hadn't come along."

"I suspect," she said, "you would have found someone else and been just as happy."

I insisted that wasn't the case, that she was the only one for me. But I now realize she was right. I know that, just as I know there are many vocations I could have happily pursued.

This is not to say God doesn't have a will or wish for our lives. Of course she does. But I've come to understand God's will as general, not specific, giving us wide latitude in our search for meaning and happiness.

"What does the Lord require of thee," the prophet Micah wrote, "but to do justly, love mercy, and walk humbly with God."

Justice, mercy, and humility are a useful rule of thumb for gauging God's will. When we live within these values, we are more likely to be living within the will of God, no matter our religion or creed.

So does God have a specific career, person, or calling in mind for you, some definite job you must undertake in order to please God? Not likely. But God does want you to serve the cause of justice, mercy, and humility as you earn your living. You can do that as a pastor, as a teacher, as an accountant, or as a ditchdigger. *It is the general will of God that you and I are called to seek out and pursue.* Are you called to have children? That is up to you. But if you do, you are called to raise them with grace, equipping them for lives of justice, mercy, and humility. Was it God's will for you to live where you do? God was neither for it nor against it. But wherever you live, God wants you to promote the ideals of justice, mercy, and humility. Was it God's will for you to marry your spouse? No, that was your decision. But having married, God's will for you is to love your partner deeply, working together for the cause of justice, mercy, and humility.

Do you see how this works? Do you see the wide freedom God has given all of us, knowing we are happiest when we are free to choose the course of our lives, constrained by only one condition, and that is this: that whatever we do, it is God's will for us to be happy and whole, while being mindful and considerate of others.

Perhaps you can't imagine the distress of those who have been told God's will is a narrow path they must discern and follow or face misery and condemnation. I have met adults well into their fifties, racked with guilt and fear at their perceived failure to obey God's will. One man I know married in his teens after his girlfriend became pregnant. Unfortunately, their marriage ended in divorce within a few years. He is lonely and wants to remarry but was told by his pastor it would violate God's will. He continues to lament his youthful indiscretion and dismisses the possibility of a second chance at happiness and love. He is utterly persuaded his sorrow and loneliness are deserved. While he has the capacity to forgive others, he lacks the ability to forgive himself, and apparently the ability to question his pastor. He believes God's will for his life was narrow and specific, and that he missed out on it.

I know another person who was sexually promiscuous as a young man. In his early twenties, he attended a revival where, racked with guilt about his sexual conduct, he became a Christian. Believing he had violated God's will for his life, he decided to become a pastor and spend the rest of his life serving God. Unfortunately, he lacks the gifts and graces for pastoral ministry and has left a trail of ruined churches in his wake. Many persons have advised him to consider other vocations more suited for his talents, but he refuses, believing ministry is God's will for his life. So instead of the world being gifted with a fine scientist or firefighter or physician, it must endure an incompetent pastor.

I think of all the people I've known who persist in loveless, demeaning marriages, unsuitable jobs, and appalling circumstances, convinced these are God's will for their lives. It would be one thing if anyone were being helped by their devotion, but the fruit they bear is often bitter, symptomatic of spiritual brokenness. While it is the case that God's will for our lives might at times make us uncomfortable, our constant misery likely indicates we have misinterpreted God's call and claim on us.

So how might we discover our life's calling? In his book *Wishful Thinking*, Frederick Buechner writes, "The place God calls you to is the place where your deep gladness and the world's deep hunger meet." Note what Buechner is saying. He is not saying our happiness is more important than the world's need. Nor is he saying the world's need is more important than our happiness. He is saying that where those two things intersect, where our work not only brings us joy but also alleviates human suffering, that is where we are called to serve.

The man who loves the practice of law but thinks only of his own enrichment is neglecting an important half of the equation. The woman who teaches in an inner-city school but resents her students is out of sync with God's will for her life. Our joy is not enough. We must consider the needs of others. But meeting the needs of others must not be our only consideration when seeking God's will. We must consider what brings us joy, too. Grouchy saints are a poor testimony for the reality of God.

Discerning the will of God isn't a grim, forced march. We are not meant to find the one narrow path through life's thicket that will lead us to a hidden treasure. We are simply invited to be God-aware and self-aware, paying careful attention to our happiness and the well-being of others. This is a joyous task, undertaken with good humor and cheerfulness. What delights us? What work do we find personally fulfilling? As we undertake it, are others also blessed? Is the world made better because of our efforts? This should be a happy, exciting exploration of life, undergirded with an eagerness to learn, grow, and help.

A woman in a Quaker meeting I once pastored had graduated from college and was determined to earn a good living. Bright and capable, she could have easily succeeded at many vocations. She was a joy to be around, and several companies wanted to hire her. Eventually, she discerned God's calling, driving a school bus for handicapped children. The work was difficult—the school district had gone through three drivers in less than a year—but when she learned of the job, she sensed she might be good at it. Of course, it didn't require a college degree, though it did require gifts no book can ever confer— compassion, sound judgment, perseverance, and good humor. She applied for the job, was hired, and drove the bus for twenty years, forming deep friendships with her students and fellow bus drivers. When I hear preachers of prosperity assure their congregations that if they follow God's wish for their lives they will enjoy prosperity, I think of my friend who drove school buses, lived modestly, and exuded joy.

Where do your joy and our world's need intersect? Does our world need another gunmaker, another hedge fund manager, another pastor to start yet another church? Don't we need people who help us care for our elderly, people who clean our cities and towns, who will help heal our broken youth and addicted adults? Don't we need inventors and creators and innovators? Can't joy and meaning be found in those important endeavors? Though our economy might not recognize the importance of such work, it is essential to a whole and happy world.

When our children are considering their life's work, do we

steer them toward some lucrative field, or do we urge them to consider careers that contribute to human well-being? When our colleges graduate thousands of engineering students each spring, are those students encouraged to use their knowledge for the benefit of all, designing and developing goods that promote human happiness? It's a sad commentary on American morality that nearly every new weapons systems developed in the past hundred years has its origins in our nation, designed by Christians who would not personally harm anyone though they invented armaments that can annihilate millions. Surely this can't be God's will.

God's plan for our lives is never a mystery, never a narrow path obscured by a tangle of overgrowth. It is found at the happy intersection of our great joy and the world's deep need. It is found where and when people are cherished and loved. It is found where the hungry are fed, where the prisoners are set free, where the poor hear good news, where light shines in the darkness, and the darkness has not overcome it.

Why It Matters

The notion that God has one narrowly defined plan for each of us lies behind many kinds of dysfunction. I know a man whose grandfather and father served as pastors, reaching prestigious positions in their denomination. When the boy was in his late teens, he came under intense pressure from his family to enter the ministry. Though he had many misgivings, he was eager to please his parents so agreed to attend college and seminary and prepare for that vocation. His father was delighted and praised his son for his willingness to do God's will.

The son studied theology in college, then enrolled in seminary, where he did well. The day he graduated, he was awarded several honors for his work. His future looked promising. He interviewed at several churches and accepted a position at an important congregation on the East Coast. Six months into his pastorate, he arrived at church disoriented. Concerned, a member of the church rushed him to a local hospital, where it was discovered he had taken illegal drugs. His family and church were shocked, his father and grandfather acutely embarrassed, especially when learning his abuse of drugs had begun in seminary.

Eager to help him, the church granted him a leave of absence and paid for his treatment at a rehabilitation facility. As was his custom, he "graduated" with honors, returned to work, and remained drug-free for the next year. His church and family relaxed, believing his drug use was an aberration, that he had learned his lesson and would remain drug-free. But one night he failed to show up for a meeting, and the next day he missed a lunch appointment. A concerned friend from the church went to his home and found him barely conscious.

The church, a bit more leery this second time, warned him that his job was in jeopardy and insisted he return for treatment, this time at his own expense. He refused, quit his job, and went to work building homes. His family was appalled and, when asked about their son, would shake their heads in sorrow.

Curiously, their son thrived. He found the work of providing housing for families meaningful. He enjoyed his co-workers, appreciating their rough-and-tumble comradery. Within a year, he was placed in charge of his own building crew and was deeply respected by those who worked under him. Drugs lost their appeal; his work supplied all the exhilaration he needed. The next year he built a small home for a schoolteacher; they fell in love and were married. Within several years, they had two children and he added a room to the home he had built.

Sadly, his father has never accepted the idea that his son chose a different course in life and sometimes asks him when he will return to the Lord's work. But the son is adamant that he is doing God's work. I hope one day his father will realize what is obvious to everyone else—that God's will for one life is not God's will for every life.

When others insist we follow their understanding of God's will, all manner of damage is done. We are shaped by a narrow and constrained view of God, and lose sight of life's wider possibilities. I have learned the will of God cannot be doggedly imposed, it can only be freely embraced. The former leads to misery, the latter to joy.

Chapter 11

___

The Contagion of Hatred

When I became a pastor, in the mid-1980s, a national Quaker service organization announced they would not discriminate against gays and lesbians in their hiring practices. This was received as welcome news by some Quakers, and as a sign of the apocalypse by others. Threats of reduced funding followed, most vociferously from persons who had never given the first dime to the organization. Nevertheless, the organization wished to honor its historic religious ties and agreed to send a spokesperson to our area to discuss the matter with concerned Quakers. The meeting was held in the home of a generous supporter, and all interested parties were invited to attend.*

The representative began by describing the lengthy process

___

* It says something about the relative size of Quakerism that all interested persons could fit inside a living room.

the organization had undergone, seeking input from Quakers and the gay community, and educating themselves about the nature of sexual orientation, in order to make an informed decision. Their decision was not made hastily or arbitrarily, and it was faithful to the Friends' discernment process, none of which mattered to those opposed to their conclusion. Despite the uproar, only a dozen or so persons attended the meeting, my first inkling that while many people will happily criticize and condemn a controversial decision, only a relative few are willing to constructively engage it.

I was unsure where I stood on the issue of homosexuality. On one level, I was uncomfortable imagining two men having sex, though to be honest imagining certain heterosexual couples making love didn't thrill me, either. I remember telling myself that I didn't understand what it means to be black, but that my lack of understanding hadn't kept me from caring about the African-American experience. With that, I went to the meeting determined to listen and, if invited, to support the organization's efforts to promote equality and inclusion. Not that my support would have been noticed at that time. I was still quite young, in a spiritual tradition that values the wisdom of elders.

Another reason I was inclined to be supportive was more personal. I was beginning to suspect my little brother was gay. Years earlier, when I had got my hands on that copy of *Playboy,* I had shown it to him, believing he would be as fascinated with it as I was. To my surprise, he showed no interest and handed it back without a word. Plus, he never talked about girls and was a whiz at home decoration. We shared a bedroom for sixteen years, and it looked like something straight out of *House Beautiful*, a copy of which he kept hidden beneath his mattress.

Arriving at the meeting, I sensed an undertone of anger. Persons who were normally outgoing and friendly were tight-lipped and serious, clearly not happy with the Quaker organization and the woman it had sent to meet with us. Our host opened the discussion by welcoming us, then introduced the representative, who thanked us for taking time out of our busy schedules to meet with her. My schedule wasn't all that busy, but I nodded as if it were—as if I would be up until midnight the next three nights making up for lost time. She passed out copies of their new hiring policy, explained how it had been created, then invited us to share comments or concerns.

Several persons, all of them belonging to the same congregation, expressed their disappointment with the organization. Their language was strong, even threatening. They feared the hiring policy would invite God's wrath upon Quakers worldwide. They predicted it would damage our credibility among potential converts, cause a precipitous decline in membership, and create a climate of hostility and division.* Others suggested the opposite might happen, that potential converts might be encouraged by the new policy. They reminded us that Quakers have a long history of tolerance and acceptance, often at great cost. They believed this was the next logical step for

---

* I have noticed those who mightily resist equality blame the subsequent division not on their own intransigence but on the "political correctness" or "liberality" of those who work against injustice. Another word for political correctness is *civility*, a virtue every person of faith should happily embrace.

a denomination that had worked for the inclusion of women, blacks, and others.

You can imagine what happened. Each group failed to change the mind of the other. After two hours, our host called an end to the gathering, thanked everyone for their participation, and we parted. Curiously, one of the men who had led the charge against the policy would, several years later, leave Quakerism and come out of the closet. It angered me at the time, interpreting his resistance as dishonest and hypocritical. But I see it differently now. Having been warned all his life about the evils of homosexuality, he felt unable to acknowledge his sexual orientation. Why would he? To do so would result in the loss of his friends as well as his church, and perhaps even the rejection of his family. Fearing this, he masked his true identity behind a façade of religious purity, until he was no longer able or willing to sustain a lie. Some of the most adamant opponents of homosexuality I have met were later revealed to have engaged in same-sex relationships. One man joined an effort to have my pastoral credentials revoked because of my support for gays and lesbians. When he died, we learned he'd had a decades-long sexual relationship with another man. I place the blame for this sad phenomenon squarely upon a church that has treated gay people with such contempt they have understandably suppressed or denied their sexual orientation.

Having lost this battle, with marriage equality now a settled matter of civil law, those same persons and churches who stoked the fires of intolerance against gays and lesbians have turned their sights on transgender people, falsely claiming they are pedophilic and predatory, despite evidence to the contrary. We seem unwilling to be persuaded by the facts if they lie outside of what we consider the norm. Over 99 percent of the time, the genitalia of a newborn match the child's brain gender. But this is not true for everyone. For these statistical few, the outward transition toward their brain gender is an ongoing process, sometimes not happening until they are well into adolescence. These people describe themselves as males trapped in a female body, or vice versa.

Other persons, again a small percentage, are born with ambiguous genitalia, possessing both male and female characteristics. They are often socialized into a specific gender, often at the preference of the parents, only to discover they have been assigned a gender they ultimately can't embrace. Regrettably, many in the church, unable to imagine a world in which some people defy their tidy categories of male and female, not only demonize such people but attempt to use the muscle of law to deny them access to the restrooms that correspond with their evolving identities.

I once asked a transgender man if he would share his story with me. He told me he was born in the 1960s with ambiguous genitalia. His parents had two sons and wanted a daughter, so they asked the surgeons to "make it a girl." As their "daughter" grew, they began to observe masculine traits in her, until finally, in "her" mid-twenties, she told her parents she felt like a man. Her parents, having long harbored the fear they had unwittingly chosen the wrong gender for their child, agreed to assist her medical and social transition. Michelle became Mike. Mike has a beard, wears flannel shirts and cowboy boots, and works construction. If Mike were to use the bathroom of the gender assigned to him at birth, as some state laws require, he would be arrested, if not beaten first by irate husbands and boyfriends.

When I say the church has opposed the LGBT community, I do not mean all the church. Fortunately, many Christians have been at the forefront of support for gay and transgender persons, so I am not suggesting all Christians are intolerant, just some. And those some ought to know better. Some of them, and I'm thinking of those Christians whose children are gay or transgender, demean and diminish the very children God entrusted to their care. It is beyond me how any parent with a gay or transgender child could reject the very essence of that child. If there is a God who judges, surely their sin of arrogance would offend that God more deeply than the supposed sin of homosexuality.

I think also of political and religious charlatans who have blamed many of our societal ills on gay people. It is not lost on me, so I'm confident it is not lost on God, that they have made their fortunes fanning flames of hatred. Their appeals to the ignorant and intolerant among us, and their utter disregard of Christian kindness, embody the very Antichrist they so frequently warn against.

As the tides of time and education lessen our cultural hostility toward LGBT persons and the river of money opposing them trickles to an end, I will be curious to see what new group will incur the wrath of these hucksters. Say what you will about Judas, at least when he forsook Jesus for financial gain, he was soon remorseful. I sense no regret among these peddlers of fear, no flickering of doubt, no reconsideration of their biases, only a doubling down of their venom and scorn.

Then there are those in the church whose opposition to

equality is rooted in their fear of institutional division. These are the peacemakers among us, the Neville Chamberlains of the religious world, who promise peace in our time if we move forward slowly, glacially, so as not to offend those in our spiritual communities who might not embrace full inclusion. These are the Christians for whom institutional cohesion is so important it trumps mercy and justice. Let me be clear, I am not speaking of those well-intentioned persons trying to be faithful to their scriptures, though I think they would be better served by studying the history and nature of religious writings. I am speaking of those who value the institution of religion above mercy and grace, who worship at the altar of some supposed unity. I suppose there might be, at least theoretically, a worldwide spiritual community united in all matters, but I've not encountered it. To pursue this fantasy of unity at the expense of the oppressed seems a poor choice to me. When will this mythical unity be achieved? When the last person resistant to equality finally dies? And how long will that take? When this mythical unity is achieved, will we look back and realize we have paid far too high a price? Will we look at the people we have silenced and sidelined and say it was worth it?

I am wary of any plan or person whose vision of unity requires ongoing discrimination against an entire class of people. No goal is so precious it should require the continued mistreatment of God's beloved. There are roughly 39,000 Christian denominations today. It is sheer folly to think we can avoid any future schisms. If divisions should arise, let it be said we parted company over an issue so central to the gospel we could do nothing less.

And why is this issue so critical? Because it is symptomatic of an underlying disease that if left to grow unchecked will fester and spread. Once we have made it acceptable to despise one group, we will soon despise another. Hatred and scorn have huge appetites, and they are never content to nibble on appetizers when they can have the whole feast. Not challenging hatred on the grounds that it will one day dissipate and dwindle is like believing that if a lion is permitted to feed once, it will require no further meals.

Fortunately, the younger generation seem unwilling to carry forward their parents' and grandparents' prejudices against gays and lesbians. This was the happy benefit of our society's awareness of sexual orientation and its causes, and the subsequent openness that knowledge encouraged. It became impossible to pretend we didn't know any homosexual people. As a pastor, I have seen resistance to homosexuality fade as people realized they had friends and family members who were gay. It was no longer possible to speak about "those people" and dismiss them out of hand. We are often able to sustain prejudices against strangers, but when those biases harm or offend those we love, we reconsider.

I have a friend who serves as a pastor in the southern United States. Theologically traditional, he joined with other pastors to resist the inclusion of gay people in their denomination. His wife shared his convictions, and they worked side by side for years to "save" their churches from this perceived menace. Their perspective was effortlessly maintained until their twenty-one-year-old son returned from college and informed them he was gay. After the initial shock wore off, they talked with their son about his sexual orientation, asking him to describe his experience as a gay man. He explained he first had feelings for other boys when he was in the fourth grade and his friends began to express interest in girls, an interest he never shared.

Gradually, because changes of heart are seldom immediate, his parents reconsidered sexual orientation, its causes, and their response. In denominational meetings, they began defending gay people, urging the church not only to welcome them but to support their right to marry. Their former allies turned on them, they lost many friends, and eventually they left their church to pastor a more inclusive fellowship. Several years later, their son found a partner and the father performed their marriage service, where he spoke movingly about his spiritual evolution on the matter. I hear from people every week who have undergone similar transformations.

Those who believe the church of the future will faithfully carry their opposition to inclusion forward will be disappointed. Time is against them. Churches that assert an antiquated and harmful theology will decrease in size, number, and cultural significance. For me, my brother, and so many wonderful people we all know, it will be a good day when the ignorance on gender and sexual orientation which masquerades as Christianity sputters to its inevitable end.

Why It Matters

When I was in junior high school, I was the World's Skinniest Boy and the occasional subject of bullying. Rather than distance myself from one of my tormentors, I tried to become his friend by laughing when he attacked someone else, grateful

I wasn't that day's target. His customary tactic was to accuse someone of being gay, then slug them in the arm or knock their books to the ground. I never challenged him, believing that as long as he was attacking someone else, I would be safe. It never occurred to me that his appetite for torment was insatiable and when he tired of picking on others, he would turn on me, which is precisely what happened one day in gym class when the teacher turned his back and my tormentor pushed me to the ground and kicked me in the face.

I was stunned, wondering why he had attacked me since I had never challenged his violence against others. I felt as if an unspoken contract had been broken, that I would not challenge his torment of others so long as I was spared. Obviously, no such contract had existed, at least in his mind. But even this realization didn't alter my relationship with him. I continued to turn a blind eye to his abuse of others, grateful to be spared, if only for a moment.

We are grown now, both of us live near our hometown, and I see him from time to time. His life has not gone well, for which he blames everyone but himself. On his Facebook page, he singles out those he believes responsible for his difficulties—gays, immigrants, people of color, liberals, and Muslims. He has spent his life verbally attacking and diminishing the "other" and is delighted when the politicians he supports vocalize their own thinly veiled disdain for those he despises.

I wonder how his life, and the lives of those he tormented, might have been better if a teacher or parent had fully appreciated the eventual consequences of his behavior. Once the maltreatment of the "other" has been tolerated, the cruelty, like a disease, will poison others. The antidote, I am convinced, is bravery in the face of malice, and our unswerving commitment to the loving treatment of all, lest the contagion of hatred fester and spread.

Chapter 12

The Cancer of Certainty

I was eighteen years old, and talking with a fundamental Baptist, when I first remember hearing the word *infallible*, though I had known the concept long before that and had attributed it to my father, whom I had been taught never to question, though I was permitted to mutter under my breath, so long as the muttering didn't descend into full rebellion. The Baptist told me Quakers were going to hell because we didn't believe in the Bible. I wasn't sure what to make of that, since we read the Bible and our pastor spoke from the Bible and there were Bibles on the backs of the meetinghouse benches next to the little cards that visitors were invited to fill out and drop in the offering plate, which they never did, fearing the pastor would visit them.

"We believe in the Bible," I told the Baptist.

"Do you believe it is the infallible, inerrant Word of God,

true in all matters, and our final and ultimate source of authority?" he asked, like Senator Joseph McCarthy grilling a communist.

"I don't think we go quite that far," I said.

"I knew it!" he cried out, delighted to have flushed out a heretic from the tall grass.

If I were starting a new religion, and forced to compete with the zillion other religions for market share, I would begin by declaring myself infallible. I would call myself He to Whom God Has Spoken and boot out anyone who questioned me. In other words, I would do what every religion known to humanity has done—invent an authority in whom all Truth resides and make anyone who joined the religion pledge allegiance to that authority.* For laughs and giggles, I would declare myself the sole interpreter of that truth, since it's my religion and I could do as I pleased and if anyone didn't like it, they could not let the door hit them on their keisters on their way out.

Indeed, there's no finer tool than infallibility to sustain the status quo, which always serves those in power and keeps them in power. Any suggestion for change, any fresh idea, any effort to reshuffle the deck hits a brick wall. *This is God's will. The Bible is clear on this matter. The tradition is without error. God has spoken. We must obey.* These pronouncements are often made with a tone of regret that suggests the speakers would change the rules if it were up to them, but alas, their hands are tied.

A close relative of infallibility is institutional inflexibility, when change is next to impossible, blocked at every turn by

---

* Infallible Truth is always capitalized.

complex, unbending procedures. In these systems, the word *infallibility* would be anathema, but the practical result is the same—a chiseled-in-stone process virtually guaranteed to halt any and all forward movement. As I write this, the United Methodist Church finds itself unable to move forward on marriage equality because of an inflexible process that permits United Methodists in Africa to block efforts toward full inclusion by United Methodists in the United States.* While United Methodists fully reject the concept of biblical infallibility, their ecclesial structure has the identical effect—the persistence of the status quo. Of course, altering the process would require the assent of those who've benefited from its cumbersome nature, so change is unlikely.

I wish I could say Quakers were exempt from this problem, but it wouldn't be true. Because we don't vote in our business meetings, instead discerning the way forward by trusting God will lead us there together, our de facto infallibility occurs when one or two Friends refuse to approve an action other Friends clearly favor. Their language, of course, is the language of holy obedience. They regret their opposition to this new measure, but the Lord has led them to take this stand. They will often cite some obscure verse of Scripture, or say

---

* It's ironic that the progressive voices, who in the previous century insisted on the full inclusion of African Christians in the church, now find those African voices raised in opposition to the inclusion of LGBT Christians. Just so you know, I am for the full inclusion of Africans, gays, trans folk, skateboarders, go-go dancers, CEOs, farmers, students, Catholics, atheists, fundamentalists, Trumpites, Clintonites, racists of every stripe and color, and everyone else, except for radio talk show hosts, who should be quarantined on an island and able to talk only to one another.

the Lord spoke to them in a dream, or quote a deceased Friend who would most certainly have opposed this change were he or she alive to do so.

The proponents of infallibility, and there are many, claim it protects the church from error, as if modern people are incapable of discerning truth so must rely on the wisdom of ancient people who believed the world was flat and seizures were caused by demons. Those who hold with infallibility are upholding a worldview uninformed by science and thousands of years of thought and reason. They have no confidence that thoughtful men and women can decide matters for themselves. *Infallibility, at its heart, is not the defense of truth, but the protection of ignorance.*

I was recently invited to speak at a church in Washington, D.C., and asked my wife if she would go with me, promising her we could see the sights. She loves walking for miles and miles in sweltering heat and staring at statues, so she agreed to go. While visiting the Jefferson Memorial—which incidentally is stunning and if you've never seen it, you need to—I saw engraved on the wall this quote from Thomas Jefferson:

> *I am not an advocate for frequent*
> *changes in law and constitutions,*
> *but laws and institutions must go*
> *hand in hand with the progress*
> *of the human mind. As that becomes*
> *more developed, more enlightened,*
> *as new discoveries are made, new*
> *truths discovered and manners and*

> *opinions change, with the change*
> *of circumstances, institutions*
> *must advance also to keep pace*
> *with the times. We might as well*
> *require a man to wear still the*
> *coat which fitted him when a boy*
> *as a civilized society to remain*
> *ever under the regimen of their*
> *barbarous ancestors.*

If ever there were a perfect argument against the presumed infallibility of people, texts, and institutions, that would be it. Infallibility simply does not permit the church to keep pace with enlightenment and discovery. It drapes us in the garb of our spiritual infancy and even as we outgrow it, forbids us from donning a garment more fitting, saying it is God's preference that we remain as we have always been. When we question those "preferences" of God, we are accused of doubt and heresy, the twin sins of the enlightened and thoughtful everywhere, and are admonished to return to the truth. Ultimately, what infallibility demands is our steadfast refusal to study matters more closely, more critically, lest the wizard behind the curtain be revealed and we discover he had nothing to do with God and everything to do with his own power.

Infallibility enshrines not only the occasional good law but the many cruel ones. When my brother was in college, he began attending a fundamentalist church that targeted homesick students. After joining the church, he was forbidden from dating anyone outside the church. Within a few months, he had a new girlfriend who, like everyone else in that congregation, blindly accepted everything told her by her pastor. I was interested in religion, starting to dabble in it myself, so I asked her to tell me about the church she and my brother attended.

"We follow the Bible," she said. "Whatever it says to do, we do."

"If your hand caused you to sin, would you cut it off?" I asked, referring to Matthew 5:30.

"Absolutely," she said, without the slightest hesitation.

She would literally take an ax and chop off her hand! Think about that.

I told her I had enjoyed our little talk, then went to my brother and suggested that he find a new girlfriend—that introducing her genes into our family line would further jeopardize an already weakened strain.

Interestingly, when I spoke with his girlfriend about other things, she was bright and witty. I could see why my brother was attracted to her. But when the conversation shifted to religion, it was as if she had been plucked from the modern era and deposited in the Dark Ages. The light went out of her. Someone, probably their goofy pastor, had convinced her the pinnacle of truth was reached thousands of years ago in the filthy, brutal hamlets of Palestine, where they stoned women accused of adultery. Why has that morally blighted era been elevated in the annals of wisdom?

Unfortunately, the fans of literalism and infallibility can't imagine any other approach to faith, can't imagine any religious alternative other than the grim road they have solemnly trod.

"So I can believe anything I want?" they ask me, thinking

they have trumped me, that the possibility of free thought is so unsupportable I'll crumple in a sobbing heap and admit the foolishness of my ways.

"Anything at all," I say. "Anything you want. And some of your beliefs about God will be silly and unhelpful, and when you realize that, you'll stop believing them. And some of your beliefs will be wise and beneficial, and when you realize that, you'll retain them."

This is beyond many of them, this notion that reasonable people are perfectly capable of discerning truth without the church taking us by the hand, as one would a toddler, and leading us to it. My advice: Shake off that hand! Find your way. If you wander down a wrong path, you will eventually discover your misstep, correct your path, and be a wiser, better person for it. You now know what doesn't work. Find your way, then test it. Share your sense of God with those whose judgment you respect. Don't worry whether they are properly ordained, or have the church's imprimatur. Care only that they are wise and gracious and cherish the freedom of others as much as their own. Care only that they read and think and listen deeply to God and others. Care only that they have learned to separate the wheat of wisdom from the chaff of ignorance.

For all its talk about knowing the truth, the church has done a spectacularly poor job of discerning it. We've simply assumed truth is passed down, unblemished, with no need for reinterpretation or reevaluation. If I started my own religion, I would make certain a mechanism was in place that would weigh the truth of religious claims. I would call it the Committee for Discernment and place the wisest, bravest souls on it, people who cared so little for power they would never insist on their own way or perspective.* They would care only for the ineffable beauty of truth, whether that truth arrived to us via religion, experience, thunderbolt, or science. Most of all, I would insist on our absolute freedom to think, explore, and discover.

When I stopped believing in hell and that God would send people there, a fellow Quaker approached me during our annual meeting, furious at my departure from the truth, or his version of it anyway.

"So anything goes?" he said. "We can do whatever we want?"

"We already can," I said. "Provided we are willing to accept the consequences of our actions."

"So nothing is right or wrong?" he asked.

"I didn't say that. There are still right things and wrong things. There is still truth. I just no longer believe the church has sole ownership of it."

And there you have it, friends. That is the crux of the matter. The champions of biblical infallibility believe God has spoken to them, has revealed truth to them, and that truth must be defended at all costs. Theirs is a disease of the heart and mind that has crushed the spirits of untold millions, snuffed out the flickering light of fresh thought and freedom, cheerfully preserved the status quo, all in the name of God. Though the Bible begins with a burst of creative life, they believe that same creative spirit has fallen silent with nothing more to say, nothing more to teach. This is the real crime of infallibility—it not only prohibits our thinking a new thought but prohibits God from offering it. Thus, infallibility might be the gravest

---

* Quakers love forming committees.

sin of all—the church telling God to be silent, that we have nothing more to learn.

There is, as far as I know, only one antidote to the diseases of inerrancy and infallibility, and that is to test all claims. Scrutinize what you are ordered to believe. Don't be cowed by vestments or stained glass or big Bibles or wealth or tradition. Recognize that the God the powers-that-be claim to follow is also available to you, that the moral teachings of Jesus and the prophets are as accessible for you as they are for them. Don't tremor when stentorian voices are raised and pulpits are pounded. Indeed, that is the time to resist, for I have learned that truth and volume are inversely related, that when the former is shakiest, the latter is loudest.

When I was eighteen and talking with the fundamental Baptist, I asked him how he could be so certain of things. I was a seeker and sincerely wanted to know what he knew and have what he had, even as I suspected we might not end up singing from the same page.

I asked him how he knew the Bible was true.

"God said it, I believe it, and that settles it," he said. We were seated at a table eating our lunch, and I remember him slapping the tabletop triumphantly as if the matter were resolved, as if we had just agreed on the price of something.

"But how do you know God said it?" I asked, genuinely curious.

"All Scripture is God-breathed and is useful for teaching, for reproof, for correction, and for training," he said.

I had read the Bible several times and recognized his response as 2 Timothy 3:16, but I told him that proving the Bible is true by citing the Bible seemed suspect to me. He said either I believed it or I didn't, which I suppose was technically true but seemed to lack the kind of theological subtlety I was coming to appreciate in my own search for truth.

I have read the Bible from front to back, studied it in college and seminary, and not just studied it but studied the culture from which it arose, studied the nature of religious texts and the process by which they were created and eventually deemed sacred. And I have to tell you, I don't for a moment believe they are the final and conclusive Word of God. They celebrate God, they point to God, and in several places they capture the vast spirit of God, if such a spirit can ever be captured, but they are not God. Not the Torah, not the Bible, not the Koran.

Truth is so robust, so vital, so immense, it could no more be contained in one book than the sun could be confined in a box. Religions can point to that truth, savor it, seek it, and celebrate it. But they can never grasp it in its entirety, or fully own or control it. No matter what they tell you. We can build our religious levees to confine the river of God, but the spirit will rise and the levees will breach. This is the way it has always been, making claims of certainty and infallibility all the more absurd. "The spirit blows where it pleases," said Jesus, who presumably ought to know.

Why It Matters

I'm writing this on the heels of an explosive event in Charlottesville, Virginia, when local authorities voted to remove a statue of Robert E. Lee from a municipal park. Enraged members of the KKK, the alt right, and neo-Nazis gathered to protest on the campus of the University of Virginia, where they met resistance from counterprotesters determined to oppose their ignorant bigotry. As I listened to the arguments from the hate-filled far right, it occurred to me their political rigidity was at its heart very similar to the religious infallibility I've experienced. Both the political and the religious inerrantists believed they were incapable of error, so were therefore impervious to reason. Nothing could be said that would dissuade them from their views.

I have no magic ball to perceive the future, but it's not difficult to see the consequences if this rigid, hateful thinking gains ground. Convinced of a reality that has no basis in fact and certain their world is at risk, they will often see violence as their weapon of choice. Whether the inerrantist is a Christian Timothy McVeigh, a radical Islamist Osama bin Laden, or a fascist Richard Spencer, they hold in common the belief in their right to silence or banish those with whom they disagree. There is no middle ground, no compromise, no resolving matters with goodwill and wisdom. They demand the world acknowledge their purity of thought, and woe to the world if it refuses.

It wouldn't surprise me to learn that all forms of an infallibility mind-set are intrinsically related. Religious certainty begets political certainty, which begets social certainty, and with that comes the perceived right to insist on one's way, at gunpoint if necessary. The absolutist abhors nuance, separating the world into saved and damned, black and white, right and wrong. While some might express their beliefs more diplomatically than others, their ultimate goals are the same—purification and if that isn't going to happen, then exclusion.

Diversity is anathema to them, a sign of concession and weakness, a caving-in.

That is why infallibility is the enemy of civil society, and should be challenged in all its forms, no matter how holy or high-placed its proponents are. It is the final refuge of the insecure and power-starved. When present in religion it endeavors to silence the other; when found in politics it does not rest until divergent voices are shouted down or exiled. It is the cancer of any healthy culture, in urgent need of a cure.

Chapter 13

————

The Spacious Life of Jesus

The Trinity, and Why It Confounds Me

As I was entering my twenties, I began dating a young lady whose father wanted to interview me to make sure I was theologically suitable for his daughter. I was a little out of practice, having not been grilled about my faith since confirmation, so was a bit confused when he asked me where I stood on the Trinity. I was familiar with the word but fuzzy on the definition, so I asked him to explain it to me. "God is one," he said, "but three. Think of an egg. It is one thing but consists of three parts—the shell, the white, and the yolk—which are inseparable."

I pointed out that my mom separated egg whites from yolks whenever she made a chocolate pie and suggested he needed a better analogy, which he didn't appreciate, and he forbade his daughter from seeing me again. Quite literally, we never saw each other again, since they moved the next week. She's not even on Facebook, which these days is the same as not existing. A few weeks after they moved, I went with a group of Quakers to visit a mosque that had been built in the same town as our Quaker meeting. Being the town's oldest church, we thought it appropriate to welcome the town's newest religion, especially after several letters to the editor appeared in the local newspaper predicting the end of Western civilization since the Muslims had arrived. I was out of town when the Quakers asked for volunteers to visit the mosque, so naturally I was volunteered. But I was curious about Islam and had always wanted to visit a mosque, so I was happy to go. The Muslims were very cordial and after describing the key tenets of their religion asked us to describe the god we believe in.

"He's like an egg," one of the Quakers said. "One, but three."

What's with all this egg stuff? I wondered.

Another one of the Quakers, an elderly woman, shook her head in disagreement. "Nonsense," she said.

The typical Quaker woman is nothing if not outspoken.

"Trinitarians would have us believe God has been known in only three ways, in creation as the Creator, in history as the Son, and in the present as the Spirit," she continued. "But God can be known in an infinite number of ways. You, for instance, believe God was known through Muhammad."

As she was speaking, I remembered a nun, probably Sister Peter Marie, describing the Trinity as God being known in three separate persons—the Father, Son, and Holy Ghost—and my being asked to repeat that at my confirmation, which I did, because my grandmother had traveled 120 miles on a bus to witness the Holy Spirit coming down from heaven to dwell in me, and I didn't want to scotch the deal and make her sad. But even as I was affirming that doctrine, I had my doubts, suspecting God is known in bunches of ways, not just three, and that telling God he could be known in only three ways was a bit like telling my dad he could be known only as a father, and not as a son or a friend or a Little League baseball coach or a husband or a Republican or a bug spray salesman. How absurd that an infinite Being could be known in only three ways!

Later, when studying theology, I was taught that doctrines were created in response to questions and mysteries. If that's the case, what existential uncertainty was the Trinity created to solve? Let's think about that. When Jesus was living, or within a few decades after his death, claims of divinity were made about him. It's unlikely Jesus ever used divine language about himself, so it's more likely his followers created divine language *about* him, then attributed it *to* him. Because monotheism was a central tenet of the Hebrew faith in which Christianity was rooted, this presented a problem, namely, how could the emerging church affirm the divine nature of Jesus while remaining true to monotheism?* But the difficulty didn't end there. Some of his followers experienced an ongoing spiritual presence that seemed to act with divine power, a holy spirit, if

---

* *Monotheism* is the kind of word theologians swoon over—lots of syllables to describe a rather simple idea, in this instance, the belief in a single God. In the old days, people worshipped many gods—rain gods, fertility gods, sun gods, fire gods, water gods, baseball gods, et cetera.

you will. Was this the spirit of Jesus, or another divine entity altogether? The church's eventual answer was *kind of* and *yes*, in that order.

I use the words *church's eventual answer* because it took three hundred years after the death of Jesus to arrive at some explanation, when nearly three hundred bishops met in Nicea in 325 C.E. and determined that Jesus and the spirit are coequal with God, begotten, not made, one in being with the Father, to quote the Nicene Creed. They used the Greek word *homo-ousios*, meaning "of one substance," since anything in Greek sounds authoritative.

To be sure, I have many friends who treasure the doctrine of the Trinity, and though I would happily grant them every freedom to affirm it, I have given up trying to make sense of it. And I know I'm not alone, for this doctrine has confounded theologians for centuries. My disillusionment with it began when it cost me a girlfriend and became more entrenched when I learned the church was so enamored with the Trinity they killed anyone who didn't believe in it. Executions have always turned me off. Beliefs should stand on their own two feet, not requiring the lopping off of heads. Indeed, it seems to me that the merit of any belief can be judged by the lengths people go to defend it. Poor, incomprehensible beliefs demand rigorous support. Defying reason and experience, they require the muscle of state and religion to maintain. Conversely, when a belief is so observably and obviously true, when it resonates with our experience, when it transcends cultures and eras, it requires no defense.

And so we have the Trinity, which since its inception, unable to stand on its own, has required the muscle of the church to endure. Its weakness, I believe, is found in the church's rush to elevate Jesus to divine status in order to raise the prestige of the church. It always helps, when launching a new religious enterprise, to claim your namesake is divine. In fact, humanity has been especially adept at God-creation. Over the millennia, we've assigned that glorious status not only to Jesus but to various emperors, founders of nations and religions, the mother of Jesus, and George Washington, who is famously depicted in the dome of the United States Capitol ascending to heaven and becoming a god. Mother Teresa is venerated as a Hindu goddess. The cult leader Jim Jones happily offered to fill that role, as did Louwrens Voorthuijzen, a Dutch eel vendor who claimed to be the resurrected body of Jesus Christ. Contrary to his theory, he died in 1968, leaving behind a handful of followers who still worship him. I saw a picture of Voorthuijzen taken in 1967, and he was wearing glasses. Don't you suppose if he were divine, he wouldn't need glasses?

Hasn't history shown that divinity is the trump card of religion, slapped down on the table to prove the superiority of one's religion? I'll see your miracle and raise it one god! What self-respecting religion wouldn't want its founder to be divine? Of course, if religions are about accessing supernatural power to gain some benefit, it makes perfect sense to create a being powerful enough to intervene on your behalf. Why bother praying to someone who hasn't the power to answer your prayers?

But if religion is more than the attainment of power and privilege, if it is the doorway into beauty and mystery and meaning, then not only is divinity unnecessary but it is an impediment, for it implies that enlightenment is beyond the reach of mortals. If Jesus was God, his compassion, insight, and healing presence flowed out of his divine status and were therefore not real possibilities for us, even though the church has told us to be like him. But if Jesus was fully human, and only that and nothing more, then his life, mercy, wisdom, and grace become real possibilities for us, too.

It would be a mistake to assume that because I don't support all the church's claims about Jesus, I don't honor his life and witness. This is like saying that since I doubt my mother's divinity, I couldn't possibly love her.

"Ah, but your mother isn't God," you might respond.

"Ah, and neither is Jesus," I would answer. "But that doesn't lessen my appreciation for him."

In fact, I would say I admire the simple goodness of Jesus's life so much I find no need to embellish his credentials. It is insecurity that causes us to inflate our own accomplishments, and the accomplishments of others. People at peace with themselves and those they love have no need to exaggerate their feats. I am at peace with Jesus, fully appreciative of his courage and grace, moved by his compassion, and stirred by his example. For me, it is not necessary to seat Jesus at the right hand of God, to defend his perfection, or to follow a star and sing his praises. It is enough to simply hold his lovely life before me and aspire to such loveliness myself. I need not venerate him as my ruler, for I have welcomed him as a friend, and he has done the same for me.

"You are my friends, if you do what I ask," he told his disciples.

This was not a high and mighty king, lording it over his subjects. Jesus was a friend to the rejected, a companion to the lonely. He embraced the sick, gave hope to the hopeless, and stood beside those the world had cast out. Kings don't do that, but friends do. So to say Jesus is my friend is to pay him the finest tribute possible. Indeed, I can think of no higher praise.

In this age of Facebook, the word *friend* has become nearly meaningless, assigned to persons we've never met, and likely never will. We address someone we've just met as *friend*. I've done it myself, as a gesture of goodwill or to win them over to my point of view. But surely there is a difference between someone who has stood with us through thick and thin and someone we know only through binary code, though we call them both *friend*.

The anthropologist Franz Boas, after living among the Eskimos, discerned they had dozens of words for the English word *snow*. Their familiarity with snow resulted in such a deep knowing they were able to distinguish among the many types of snow. Perhaps that is also true with our use of the word *friend*, so that when we say "Jesus is my friend and I am his," we know that means something richer than when we say "That woman is my friend on Facebook."

To be friends with Jesus is to strive for this deeper knowing, based not on fear or worship but on love. Our love for the way of Jesus inspires us to share his priorities, even when, perhaps especially when, it is most difficult. This love empowers us to reject the idols of nationalism, power, and wealth, which is always difficult, so it is naturally something we avoid. When Jesus was promoted from teacher to God, from friend to ruler, we told ourselves we could not be like him, that his way of living was possible only because of his status. But when he is one of us, we have no such excuse. What he did, we can do. He said so himself, assuring his disciples they would do greater things than he had done. Kings keep their subjects at a distance, confirming their lowliness. True friends elevate those they love, delighting most of all when their friends surpass their own gifts and graces. Jesus is not our king. He is much more. He is our friend.

Can I share another concern about Trinitarian theology? After all, we've gone this far, and I realize it might be difficult to hear criticism of what many consider to be the linchpin of Christian faith, but these things I have unlearned merit our consideration, so let me share another concern. In asserting the divinity of Jesus, we have simultaneously ruled out the possibility of God working through other faiths and persons. Is it possible that the doctrine of the Trinity, intending originally to buttress the emerging Christian faith and give it credence in the marketplace of religions, has led to spiritual arrogance? Has it caused many Christians to see themselves as members of an exclusive faith, open only to those who affirm the unique status of Jesus? How ironic that a doctrine about Jesus is so inconsistent with his personality. This is the effect of many doctrines. Even when their intent was constructive, their consequences were often negative. This is why, as painful as it might be, doctrines must be regularly examined, to see whether they continue to serve the purpose first imagined, and whether there were unforeseen adverse effects.

In reflecting on the doctrine of the Trinity, we must ask ourselves if it has outlived its usefulness. Are there ways to affirm the life and witness of Jesus that don't diminish the value of other faiths? Aware of the historical tendency of religions and nations to claim divine status for their founders, are we willing to reconsider this doctrine of exclusivity? Once we realize claims of divinity are not unique to Jesus but have been a constant theme throughout history, both before and after Jesus, how can we continue to assert that our doctrine of divinity is true and others are false? What proof is there that Jesus was any more divine than Romulus and Remus, the mythical founders of Rome? Historically, any such doubts have been met by a doubling-down, a steadfast refusal to admit a doctrine has outlived its usefulness. But if the Christian faith is committed to truth, which John the gospel writer said would set us free, then aren't we called to examine our religious claims critically and fearlessly, no matter where they might lead?

I can't help but wonder if this might be why so many young people reject the church's religious claims. Steeped in the scientific advances of the past century, they'd discovered "the heart cannot worship what the mind rejects," as the Episcopal bishop John Shelby Spong so eloquently observed. Our customary response has been to chide them for their lack of faith, when we should applaud their integrity. Perhaps we should apologize for insisting they believe things taught on Sunday that contradict what they learned Monday through Friday. Any religion which consciously and constantly divorces itself from reality and truth cannot endure. At the very least, it will not capture the minds and hearts of wise and thoughtful people. It will be a religion for the superstitious and uninformed. It will become a tribal religion, ultimately held by a relative few, and not a universal faith, under whose shade people will gather to love and learn.

Why It Matters

Like many of the teachings I have had to unlearn, the Trinity's problems lie not just in its lack of reason but in its tendency to diminish the worth and value of other religious traditions, which in this day and age can have catastrophic consequences. To assert that Jesus was divine but Muhammad, Buddha, or Confucius was not is to create a hierarchy of religions at whose pinnacle Christianity resides. While Christians might enjoy this supremacy, it is all too clear the people of other faiths don't. Spiritual hubris has caused some Christians to insist on the conversion of others, with little regard for their native faith.* The contempt for other traditions contributes to Christian arrogance and creates ill will when families and communities become spiritually fractured.

The core of good religion is mutuality, not superiority. It invites people to labor together in the transformation of our world. Essential to this cooperation is our rejection of preeminence. Isn't this consistent with the way of Jesus, who stood beside others, not above them? Our religious doctrines should meet this simple test: Does this doctrine elevate my religion over others, or does it promote mutual love, appreciation, and respect?

---

* And here I'm thinking of the Crusades and their modern-day equivalent of sending missionaries to foreign lands to tell their inhabitants they are going to hell.

To be sure, one can cite Bible verses that argue for the unique superiority of Jesus, but it is possible to view those texts as snapshots along the road of understanding, capturing a specific moment or mind-set but not so rigidly held that no other understanding is ever possible.

We must bear in mind that our surrendering of a long-held doctrine in no way diminishes Jesus. There are myriad ways to honor our spiritual teachers without denigrating the value of other teachers. We can still appreciate and honor Jesus's wisdom, compassion, and spiritual vision without insisting upon his unique superiority. As we extend respect to other faiths, we discover it is returned to us, and that the prospects for goodwill and peace are increased.

A man in my Quaker meeting married a woman of the Baha'i faith. Central to the Baha'i tradition is a high regard for the founding figures in all religions. This warm acceptance is evident in the life of this woman, who moves easily across religious boundaries, honoring the best each tradition has to offer. Her gracious esteem for others seems utterly consistent with the way of Jesus, at least as I understand it. Early in our friendship, she asked me if I minded her attendance at our Quaker meeting, since she was a Baha'i. I assured her that if all Baha'is were like her, I would be delighted if she brought a dozen more with her. And when they arrived, I would insist on no declaration of faith or unique elevation of Jesus. I would only marvel at their ability to glean from Jesus what they could and ask them to help me expand my own capacity to love and appreciate other faiths more deeply than I do, thereby honoring the spacious life and witness of Jesus.

Chapter 14

Truth Is Seldom Simple

Quakers, I have learned over the years, love nothing more than hashing out some great existential riddle, and they are perfectly content, nay delighted, to leave questions unanswered until truth decides to make itself known, if ever it does. When I first became a Quaker, this annoyed me no end. I remember beginning my learned comments with helpful phrases like "It's simple. . . ." or "I think it's obvious that . . ." or "Anyone ought to be able to see that . . ." I was especially happy when I could reduce some complex matter to a short, pithy saying and declare the issue settled.

Wiser folks in the room would smile and suggest I wrestle with matters a bit longer. Time provides a richer understanding, they would say. Life and truth aren't always easy.

But why? I wondered. I believed then that truth was simple. Indeed, the greater the truth, the simpler it was, I would say, loudly and often. It says something about the patience of Quakers that I was never discovered unconscious behind the meetinghouse, conked on the noodle.

Still often guilty of it myself, I notice when others brush off complex and difficult matters with simple proverbs—the tendency to seek the easiest explanations for life's mysteries, tragedies, and complications. No doubt we want to make sense of a world that feels senseless. Especially if we have gone to great lengths to order our lives, believing uniformity and organization will somehow protect us from chaos and harm. When we are visited with difficulty, or our worldview proves inadequate to the current hour, we seek solace in familiar sayings and proverbs, retreating to the patterns some elder or greeting card company assured us are true. We cite stories that confirm our maxims, believing if something is true in one case, it must surely be true in every case.

Many of the sayings are attributed to the Bible, though you can search high and low and not find them there. Of course, this alone doesn't diminish their value. There are many worthwhile proverbs not found in Scripture. What makes some sayings so particularly destructive is that at first glance they seem so profound, so beyond reproach, they are accepted as gospel truth, mostly because they affirm what we wish were true. *God helps those who help themselves,* or *God never gives us more than we can bear,* or that tired old chestnut that makes me want to scream every time I hear it—*Hate the sin but love the sinner.*

Perhaps we are fond of catchy sayings because religion deals with profound matters. Seeking and searching are required to find our way ahead. There is no doubt that proverbs, which are often anecdotally true, are comforting, but they often don't bear up under close scrutiny.

Let's examine each of these sayings, beginning with *God helps those who help themselves*. I used to keep this one within handy reach, retrieving it whenever I had enjoyed some little success for which I wanted credit. On one occasion, while I was in my early forties, a writing contract I had with a publisher was terminated over theological differences. To be accurate, I referred to them as theological differences, while my publisher referred to them as heresy and fired me. I immediately went to work looking for a new publisher and didn't stop until I found one. As people learned of my dismissal and quick recovery, they would often comment how God had taken care of me. I would smile, believing a display of piety was an appropriate response for a minister. But I would think, God helps those who help themselves.

As I reflected on that saying, I realized it was attractive because it affirmed the value I place upon work and personal initiative. Then a friend of mine told me just the opposite is true—God helps those who can't help themselves. God comes to the aid of the helpless, she insisted. She cited a number of stories from the Bible to confirm God's help for the helpless and made a very compelling argument. To confuse matters, another friend of mine told me there was no proof God helps those who help themselves, or those who can't help themselves. If there is a God, he said, there is no evidence that God intervenes to help anyone. For proof, he pointed to the record of history: war, starvation, grinding poverty, brutal oppression, and endemic injustice. I struggled to refute his logic, and in time became more hesitant to claim divine assistance for myself when those around me clearly were playing by the same rules but hadn't experienced that same support.

There are, of course, those who tell us if we don't acknowledge God's assistance, God will withdraw it, as if God is some petulant child who must be praised lest he throw a tantrum and take his ball home. But I believe God is pleased by sensitivity, and that it is unkind to dance with joy to the tune of someone else's dirge. If we do believe God has intervened to help us, we shouldn't forget our condition before God's help and remember others are still in that condition. To celebrate our delivery in their presence while they remain shackled with hardship is uncharitable. So, yes, God might well help us when we can't help ourselves, but there is mystery here, and a timing we don't understand, so humility and modesty are in order.

What about *God never gives us more than we can bear*? Have you ever been told that? How did it make you feel? In this life, people suffer deeply, in ways that make little sense to us. A woman I know lost four children in an automobile accident, another friend had three children perish in a house fire, yet another was let go by a company he'd faithfully served twenty-eight years, lost his home, lost his retirement, and avoided homelessness only by the skin of his teeth. Each of these three people was told by others, "God never gives us more than we can bear."

At first glance, it's comforting to think God trusts our ability to overcome life's difficulties, that God is aware of our suffering and will intervene before we are overwhelmed. I suspect those who say it believe it is true and intend it as a comfort. It also seems clear they have given little thought to their words, which are absurd when examined. If it were true God never gives us more than we can bear, no one would ever be hospitalized for depression, anxiety, or mental trauma. No one would ever be so overwhelmed by life they would lose all sense of right and wrong and take another's life. No one would commit suicide, or turn to alcohol or heroin to beat back their despair.

Some have claimed it isn't God who gives us more than we can bear but the devil. They believe a fallen angel named Satan actively attacks the faithful in an effort to destroy their lives. In response, they have developed spiritual rituals to cast out demons involving prayer, Bible reading, and exorcisms. A man I know is one of a handful of Roman Catholic priests officially recognized as an exorcist. He tells about encountering a number of demons over the years who've taken up residence in people. This sounds like nonsense to me, except I know this priest and have found him to be thoughtful and well grounded. I wish he were a lunatic so I could more easily dismiss his claims.

But I would be interested in knowing if he believes God is all-powerful and all-loving. Because if God were, then why would God permit the lives of some people to be devastated by demonic forces? My hunch is this: Sometimes evil seems so real, intentional, and systemic we attach a personality to it. That personality gives a form and shape to evil, helps us name the "enemy" while conveniently allowing us to blame evil on an otherworldly being, thereby exonerating our own complicity with it. It is, of course, a far easier matter to "exorcise" demons from another than it is to change ourselves.

I don't know if supernatural beings, either God or Satan, involve themselves in our lives. I know what other people believe, but I myself have not reached a definitive conclusion. I can offer anecdotal evidence that both supports and denies supernatural involvement. I do know complex matters like this one defy simple explanations. No saying, no matter how witty or clever, can adequately address this issue, and to act as if it does is to heighten the spiritual damage we inflict on others when we breezily claim God assisted one person but not another, or Satan tormented one while sparing another.

What intrigues me is how quickly we claim divine blessing with so little thought. A woman recently told me she had several errands to run in a hurry, so she prayed God would open a parking space near the door of the grocery store. Lo and behold, she arrived at the store and found an empty spot in the front row. I could tell she wanted me to affirm her belief in God's intervention, but I told her I would need more evidence. I mentioned that the day before I had sat with a young woman dying of cancer and thought it strange that God would find one woman a parking space while letting another woman die of cancer.

Think of it. We live in a world of 7.5 billion people, on one planet among trillions of planets in the universe. The notion that God would go out of her way to find a Christian a parking spot close to the store is fascinating. That would be like my intimately knowing each blade of grass in the world and reordering the universe to make sure particular ones were never trimmed. Say all you want about a personal God knowing every hair on our heads, this level of intervention is beyond comprehension. It's not that God doesn't give us more than we can bear, it's that the universe isn't ordered in a way that will prevent harm to everyone and everything. Besides, what is bad news to one is often good news for another. The blade of grass clipped in my hayfield might feel abandoned by God, but the cow that eats it seems to delight in the situation.

Absolute claims of divine or satanic intervention are risky. Our world provides ample evidence that both are possible, or quite impossible, depending on our perspective. To defend supernatural intervention because it happened to me is to assert that my experience is authoritative in a way the experiences of others are not. Satan might not mind such arrogance, but if the example of Jesus can be trusted, I believe God favors humility.

Finally, there's the little gem *Hate the sin but love the sinner.* I first began hearing it when Pat Robertson and Jerry Falwell realized there was money to be made warning the rest of us about gay people. Nothing fills the coffers of televangelists quicker than dark warnings of sinister homosexuals out to molest our children, ruin our nation, and destroy our marriages. Of course, to do the job effectively they had to demonize gay people, which troubled some in their audience, who had discovered they were related to gay people, or had gay friends, or were actually gay themselves. Finding it difficult to hate the people to the degree Falwell and Robertson preferred, they decided to hate the sin instead and began saying, "We hate the sin, but we love the sinner."

I remember, back in the 1980s and '90s, when my own denomination was discussing homosexuality and someone would invariably stand and say rather piously, "Let's not forget we're to love the sinner but hate the sin." They would then suggest some draconian measure to make the lives of gay people miserable and sit down, pleased with their public display of tolerance. Occasionally, they would have us believe that saying could be found in the Bible, though I could never find it. If the remark were intended to make gay people feel loved, it fell woefully short. No gay person I knew got the warm fuzzies after hearing it. What they felt was contempt and judgment. And they were all curious, as was I, about why this saying was never applied to those who were proud, greedy, lustful, gluttonous, wrathful, envious, or slothful. I have never, not once, heard it said of a short-tempered or materialistic person, "We're to love the sinner but hate the sin." Nor have I ever known such people to be barred from membership in the church or asked to leave a church once these "sins" were known.

Could you imagine the outcry if the church said to an obese person, "It appears you've been gluttonous, which according to the Bible is a sin, so you can't join the church until you renounce gluttony and lose weight." Or said to a wealthy person, "We suspect you might have a problem with greed. You live in a house far grander than your needs and appear to have accumulated too much wealth. Before we can welcome you into the church, you'll have to seek forgiveness for your greed, give your money away, and pledge to live more simply."

Instead, it appears we hate the sin and love the sinner only if we're speaking about homosexuality. And how magnanimous we appear, how generous of spirit we seem when we say it, as if we deigned to love someone we otherwise thought detestable, as if loving gay people were spiritually extravagant, when what they really deserved was our scorn. I won't even mention (well, maybe I will) how absurd it is to condemn someone's sexual orientation, which they most certainly didn't choose, as a sin.

The pattern here is plain. When confronted with complex matters requiring careful thought and nuanced understanding, the church has too often resorted to simple sayings, couched in religious terms, that do harm to truth. I've learned to beware of any religious leaders who tell me truth is simple. What they are really saying is that they are unwilling to do the hard work necessary for emotional and spiritual growth, dismissing out of hand the disciplined thought essential for moral maturity.

Such leaders might draw huge and passionate followings today, but I believe history will not judge them favorably.

Why It Matters

Because our world is so complex and challenging, it's only human to be drawn to the answers that are simple and strike us as self-evident. For the same reason, we often favor spiritual answers that don't require deep reflection, especially when those answers support our biases. For instance, if we are wealthy, isn't it tempting to believe our wealth is a direct consequence of our work ethic? Then isn't it all too easy to assume the poor are lazy? And having settled that matter, why should we bother to think more deeply about poverty, its myriad causes, and what we might do to alleviate it? This is the consequence of simplistic religion, politics, and worldviews. We seize the first and easiest "answers" and look no further.

I notice something of a correlation between the prominence of religious fundamentalism in a community and the prevalence of social ills. Do you? I can't help but wonder whether a preference for simplistic answers prevents the thorough reflection essential to progress. Too often, problems are addressed by attempting to pray them away or are declared to be God's will and therefore beyond human solutions. Consequently, social inequities can go unaddressed, only endured in grim, unquestioning "faith." But at least the devout are off the hook.

I know a woman who serves as a physician for a large Amish population in the Midwest. Because the Amish intermarry, they are far more likely than the general population to suffer from genetic anomalies and are prone to certain illnesses, many of which are physically devastating. She tells me her advice to expand their marriage pool is ignored. Whatever happens to them is God's will, they tell her, even as their children and grandchildren suffer from disorders that could easily have been avoided.

Our fondness for simple truth can be even more disastrous, especially when we too quickly embrace cultural myths that denigrate minorities, foreigners, or people of other faiths. I once attended a speech given by a politician who said he would lose no sleep if America dropped a nuclear bomb on Iran. When challenged, he defended his statement by claiming Islam was a threat to civilization, as if every Muslim were a terrorist, deserving of death. He made no effort to understand the Iranian culture, Muslim theology or history, or the moral consequences of such an action. In his knee-jerk world, the only good Iranian was a dead Iranian. This perspective follows a pattern. Tyrants gain power by first convincing us the answers to our challenges are simple. They caution us not to overthink matters, declare that the truth is obvious. They ridicule the more thoughtful and reflective among us, dismissing them as elitists or out of touch. Having turned public opinion against the wiser voices, they proceed to "solve" our problems, often through violence. When those solutions carry religious overtones, they even appear spiritually virtuous, as if they were fighting on God's behalf.

Those who insist that life and truth are simple do us no favors. They demand we surrender our God-given capacity to reason and think, thereby crippling our ability to engage life more deeply. There are many adjectives we can use to describe life, but *simple* isn't one of them. To pretend otherwise is to set ourselves up for misery and disappointment when life proves difficult, which it inevitably will. Happiness is found not in ease of life but in our acceptance of life's complexity and our determination to face it with faith, courage, good humor, and wisdom.

Chapter 15

Sacred Change

Then I Was Told God Doesn't Change and Neither Should We

When I began writing and speaking, some twenty years ago, a veteran of the trade told me if I had three good speeches, I could make a living as a speaker.

"I've been giving the same three speeches for thirty years," he said.

"Does that mean you haven't changed your mind, or that you've changed your mind but just aren't telling people?" I asked.

"I've not changed my mind and you shouldn't, either," he said. "It'll kill your career as a speaker. It alienates your fan base."

I change my mind on a regular basis, so I was unable to follow his advice. In fact, I've given speeches one week I disagreed with the next. Once, in the middle of a speech, I realized a flaw in my logic, promptly changed my mind, and had to abandon my script and wing it.

How do we go through life without ever changing our minds?

I occasionally meet an elderly gent who got religion when he was seven years old and has believed the exact same thing for eighty years. People pat him on the back and commend him for his faithfulness, and all I want to do is shake him and say, "Seriously? You haven't had a new thought in eighty years? Don't be so lazy."

In the interests of full disclosure, I must tell you that my wife has suggested I am similarly entrenched on certain matters.

But why is rigid thought seen by so many as a religious virtue? I can't think of another field in which intransigence is so prized. If our doctor didn't read another word after graduating from medical school, we would find another doctor. If an astronomer didn't let her understanding of the cosmos change after the images from the Hubble Space Telescope were published, we'd rightly conclude she was no longer a credible authority on the cosmos. But let a Christian hold fast to his old-time religion, and we will applaud his lethargy and seek his opinion on matters of faith. When he dies, we will laud his refusal to change and urge others to emulate him. Though he has not exercised a single brain cell to advance our understanding of God and has happily let the moss of tired thought cover his intellect, we will admire his unchanging faith.

If someone should come along who challenges our perceptions of God, and invites us to consider ultimate matters in a fresh light, we will wail and gnash our teeth, condemning their curiosity as injurious to our faith. (I know this is true, because I have done it myself.) We will insist they pose a threat to the church's well-being and behave as if demons from hell are battering down God's gates. We will thunder that God doesn't change, quote Scripture as conclusive proof, and fight change tooth and nail. There is no field so impervious to change as religion, and not just impervious to change but so violently opposed to change we will kill those whose ideas of God differ from our own.

In 2003 a friend of mine, James Mulholland, and I wrote a book asserting God loves humanity more extensively than the church has traditionally claimed. The book, *If Grace Is True: Why God Will Save Every Person,* generated a great deal of controversy and landed me in hot water, in the process selling a fair number of copies. Consequently, whenever I speak somewhere, someone will invariably raise a hand and comment on that book, often favorably, since the people who hate the book usually don't come to hear me speak. But those who like the book will often ask what I think about heaven.

My current answer is something like this:

I am reluctant to say anything about the afterlife, since I haven't yet experienced it. In the past I have written and spoken too conclusively about things I can't know for sure. If there is a heaven, that's fine. But I don't need it. This life has been heaven enough for me. There are many people who have suffered greatly. If there is a heaven for them when they die, that would be wonderful. But giving me heaven is like tipping a millionaire. Give it to someone else. I have enough.

It is a clear and honest answer, so in that sense it is the

most appropriate response I can make, but it often annoys people, some of whom remind me what I wrote years before, as if I've forgotten.* They then suggest that changing my mind is somehow unfair.

"But that's not what you said in 2003," they point out.

I tell them I've changed my mind, and that they are free to change their minds, too. I have changed my mind about a number of things through my life. I once dated a young woman and we discussed marriage but then changed our minds. She married someone else, and they're still together and happy. A few years later, I met a woman who then changed her mind about the man she was dating in order to date me. We eventually married and remain blissfully together. None of this happiness would have happened if we had lacked the capacity to change our minds.

It is our capacity for change that makes happiness and meaning possible. Were we unable to revise our lives or alter our thinking, were we unwilling to unlearn certain beliefs so we could embrace new ones, we would be slaves, chained to mind-sets and circumstances that no longer make us happy. Whenever religions demand our continued affirmation of creeds, traditions, and beliefs, they sign their own death warrants, for they are simultaneously forbidding the life-giving energies of adaptation, evolution, and growth.

Let's examine a bit further a belief I once held dear that I no longer find meaningful. At one time in my spiritual journey

---

* It might be a clear and honest answer, but it took me nearly twenty years to arrive at it and I still find it difficult to say it aloud.

it was vitally important for me to believe that heaven exists and that everyone is going there. A belief in universal salvation seemed the only way I could move away from the provincialism of my evangelical faith. But eventually I became just as rigid about universalism, dismissing those who disagreed with me. *It's ironic how doors that once opened our minds become gates that close them.*

After a while, it occurred to me I was most dogmatic about the one aspect of the spiritual life no one had experienced. No one had ever produced irrefutable evidence of an afterlife. Oh, sure, I had heard stories of some kid passing out for a few minutes, then being revived and telling his mom and dad he had seen his dead aunt Martha chatting with Jesus. So they took him to a Benny Hinn revival, where he told his story and everyone cried and shouted "Hallelujah!" and someone from Hollywood made a movie about it and the kid got a zillion dollars before he admitted he made it all up, so that is probably not conclusive proof of an afterlife.

But I could be wrong.

Still, it strikes me as peculiar that we in the church are most resistant to change when it denies us an advantage, like going to heaven or being healed or getting a tax break. I once spoke at a gathering of ministers who were kvetching about the national debt, so I suggested we tax church property so the debt could be lowered. It turned out the one thing they hated more than our national debt was the church paying its share of it. So one could argue that it isn't *change* that bothers us but rather our *change in status* we find most troubling.

At the heart of all change lies the unspoken realization that something we once valued is no longer central to our lives. But isn't that true throughout life? We shed the old to make way for the new. Our lives today bear little resemblance to our lives thirty years ago. Our families have expanded or shrunk. Our vocations, habits, and hobbies are no longer the same. For some of us, even our beliefs about God have changed. In my late teens, I was a Bible-believing fundamentalist. Not for long, for only a year or so, just long enough to alienate my friends and family. Today, I am more likely to be spiritually moved by holding my granddaughter than by reading the Bible.

I'm not a social scientist and can't cite any study or research, but based on my experience as a pastor, I find people whose religious beliefs never change seem to be crippled by all change. A job loss, a move, a divorce, or an illness tends to have a paralyzing effect on them. Of course, we are all affected by significant shifts in our lives, but those of us who are religiously rigid seem especially immobilized when our circumstances change. Unable or unwilling to alter that which is central to our lives, we become incapable of any change. This might explain our fascination with political movements that promise a return to the good old days.

What made the good old days so alluring was their predictability. Because we have lived through them, they are now familiar terrain, unlike the present and future, which are unknown and unpredictable. But the good old days weren't good when we experienced them. They were filled with anxiety and uncertainty. Only their familiarity makes them more appealing. When my mother-in-law was alive she would reminisce about her life during the Depression and World War II, tell stories of great hardship and suffering, then sigh contentedly and say, "We were so happy." My hunch is they were happy only in retrospect.

While there's nothing wrong with looking back fondly at our past, doing so often prevents us from being happy in the present, which is why those who dislike change are often miserable, since happiness isn't possible when it depends upon the world not changing. It's like my not being happy until I can be a child again. I will never recapture that era, so to base my happiness on an impossibility is pointless. If we are to find happiness, we must find it in the present and future, even though they are unknown and unpredictable. This means we must not just *accept* change but *welcome* change if we want to be happy.

I knew an elderly couple whose declining health necessitated a move from their home into an assisted-living apartment. The woman, eager to make new friends and have someone else cook and clean, welcomed the move. She went from room to room, selecting the pieces of furniture and artwork they would take to their new apartment and gifting the rest of their belongings to family and friends.

Her husband was infuriated by their move and did nothing to help, sabotaging his wife's efforts and, when that didn't work, exploding in anger and insisting he was staying put. His wife moved to their new home while he continued living in their old house, until he grew tired of preparing his own meals and finally joined her. But the entire time he lived in the assisted-living center, he pouted and bemoaned his altered circumstances. When he died, his family seemed relieved, if not secretly glad.

How often are we like that man, having to be tugged and

pulled into new life, which is ironic, given how often we talk about the new life Jesus offers. One would never guess we were advocates of a new anything, given our resistance to change. We make poor advertisements for the possibility of transformation. When challenged we dredge up a Bible verse or two to defend our intransigence, leading people to believe God is as grouchy and unbending as we are.

It sounds snarky when I say it like that, but some things should be named outright. Too many people join the Christian faith hoping to stave off cultural progress as long as possible. They accept Jesus into their lives, then do all they can to make sure the transformative values of Jesus don't take hold in the culture, confusing nostalgia for faith, and progress for sin. When others embrace change and move forward in a spirit of acceptance, they are castigated for caving in to the world.

Can you imagine tying your happiness to an unchanging world? Nothing guarantees our sadness more than our unwavering commitment to the past. I know a man who had modest success as a college basketball player. He's now in his sixties, has been through several marriages, is emotionally distant from his children and grandchildren, and has had difficulty keeping a job. He is most alive when talking about his college days. I'm careful never to mention the subject of sports in his presence, because he'll get cranked up and I'll be trapped for hours. It is clear he peaked early, and the rest of his life has been lived in the long shadows of his past.

If we are honest, we'll acknowledge that some churches live in the shadows of our past, when Christianity was a dominant feature of our landscape. On Sunday morning, churches were filled to the brim. On Friday evenings, when I would watch movies at the Royal Theater, a message flashed on the screen before the previews—ATTEND THE CHURCH OF YOUR CHOICE THIS SUNDAY! No one thought it odd. But all this began to change as I grew older. There were still vestiges of the church's heyday, but nothing like before. Churches once packed to the rafters were down to thirty attenders. Seminaries once overflowing with students were closing or merging, short on dollars, low on scholars.

Today, some church services feel more like funerals, one lament after another of what used to be but is no more. While some have taken this development in stride and adjusted to our new reality, others have become angry, condemning a culture that no longer hangs on their every word. There are many reasons for our waning influence, but I suspect the chief one might be our growing irrelevance. We are like the man who peaked early, so fixated on the past he failed to contemplate his future, so unwilling to leave his old reality he didn't prepare for his new one.

Too many of us believe a return to the past will restore our fortunes, so consequently reject progress and change. Just when adaptability is most necessary, we dig in and refuse to budge. Ironically, those of us most resistant to change are most likely to identify ourselves as faithful. But it takes no faith to remain entrenched in the same tired land. It is the faithful who venture forward, and the fearful who remain behind. It has always been so.

Say what you will about the beauty of tradition, and it can be beautiful, if the church is to thrive, we must create new beauty, new meaning. This needn't, and shouldn't, mean we jettison the basic values of our faith. It does mean we make careful distinction between those values and the cultural layers we've allowed to accumulate that serve little purpose. Especially when those layers have everything to do with our own power and little to do with God. This future church should transcend political parties, denominations, cultures, nations, races, and eras. It should be fluid and supple, open to innovation, engaging and transforming modern life. Because it values truth, the church of the future should be a friend to science, even as science deconstructs those mysteries and activities once attributed to God. It should delight the church to have future generations correct the fallacies of past generations, especially when those errors clouded our vision of God.

Rather than construct sacraments that require the affirmation of ancient beliefs and applaud those persons who bow to them, we should encourage the exploration of spiritual territory yet unmapped. We should be delighted when a Christian studies with a Zen master or incorporates Native American stories into worship. As Islam struggles to rise above the fanaticism which has blemished its name and reputation, we should be grateful for those Christians who find common ground with our Abrahamic kin. We should promote wide participation in America's political scene, urging bright and thoughtful Jews, Hindus, Buddhists, Muslims, Christians, pagans, and nonbelievers to political service. I believe current events bear me out when I say that when people are empowered, when they are given a say, they are less likely to abuse power or resort to violence. Rather, they want to nurture and strengthen the democratic process that sought to include them.

The church's lust for power, coupled with its insistence on right thinking, has created a community ill suited for its transformative mission. Enthralled with the powers and principalities of this world, we are unable to transcend them. Just as Jesus challenged religion's tendency toward legalism, so must we not mistake faithfulness to doctrine for faith itself. *We are not called to a rigid creedal purity, or to worldly power, but are invited to a fluid and flowing compassion capable of giving birth to cultures of peace and justice.*

I do not believe Jesus intended to start a new religion, but I do believe any religion based on his teachings should mirror his spirit of curiosity, compassion, and capacity for change. We are called, after all, to be new beings, transformed by Christ's presence in us. Thus, change is nothing to fear, or to avoid. It is the inevitable result of hearts open to life.

Why It Matters

Early in my ministry, a man in the congregation I served applied to be a member of our church. He was well into his eighties, had been raised in a bigoted family, and still retained the prejudices of his childhood, especially against people of color. When I visited him to discuss membership, he freely admitted that he had been a member of the Ku Klux Klan and commented that the KKK had done much good. I asked him if he was still a member. He said he wasn't sure, that the local group had disbanded some years before. I told him that membership in the KKK was incompatible with membership in the church, and that if he wished to be a church member, he must renounce his affiliation with the KKK and embrace the ethos of the gospel.

Initially, he refused, but we continued to visit, speaking very frankly with each other about our views on race and God. As you can imagine, our views on God also differed. The God he spoke about was judgmental and condemnatory. Why this man seemed so fond of a tyrannical deity was a mystery to me, but there's no making sense of some beliefs. Though I couldn't for the life of me understand why, the man still attended church. A year or so later he was diagnosed with terminal cancer. Interestingly, some of his caregivers were African-American and Hispanic. I suspect this was the first time he had actually met people different from himself. I began to notice a softening of his attitudes, toward others and toward God. Several months before he died, he expressed a desire to join the church. "I'm a changed man," he promised me. "I was wrong."

At one time, I might have told you an old dog can't learn new tricks, but I have been amazed at our capacity for growth and change, especially when we are able to move beyond our love affair with the past.

Since I don't own a crystal ball, it's impossible for me to predict the effect Donald Trump's presidency will have on our nation and world. What is clear is that his ascendency to power was possible because of his pledge to return America to its gloried past. I needn't mention that America's past wasn't so glorious for women, people of color, sexual minorities, and the poor. But it's clear Trump appealed to a number of people whose cultural memory was overly nostalgic. A good number of them self-identified as evangelical Christians, who were apparently willing to overlook his crude language, his history of divorces and affairs, his maltreatment of women, his dishonesty in business, his scorn for the foreign-born, and several other tendencies incompatible with Christianity. What could possibly have caused so many of his supporters to look the other way if not their fear of change, especially when they believed that change imperiled an advantage they had enjoyed?

An irrational fear of change is almost always accompanied by injustice, when we insist familiar customs be adhered to even as they harm others. To be Christian means, at the very least, that our preference for the status quo doesn't come at the expense of the poor and powerless. Doggedly insisting upon traditions that bless us and curse others is the antithesis of Jesus Christ, who is honored not by our stubborn commitment to the past but by our faithful determination to lift the lowly and give the voiceless a song to sing.

Chapter 16

The God Remaining

A friend of mine, while in college, was invited to attend a Bible study sponsored by a fundamentalist church. Hungry for community and searching for meaning, he embraced Christianity with the fervor common to new converts. He joined the church, married a woman who also belonged, and devoted a dozen years of his life to the church, spending most evenings with fellow members in Bible study and fellowship. A dozen years later the church imploded when the founding pastor had a sexual affair with a woman member. Disillusioned, my friend and his wife quit the church and have not returned to any church since. Though their passion for organized religion has waned, their belief in the Bible and its inerrancy has not.

My wife and I occasionally join my friend and his wife for dinner. When we do, our table conversation often turns to religion. He is mystified by how I can be a pastor without believing in the Bible's inerrancy and has expressed dismay that Quakers would permit such a thing to happen. He has told me, more than once, that pastors in his former church had to publicly affirm their belief in the Bible's authority before they were allowed to serve. I point out that a public affirmation of faith in the Bible didn't stop his pastor from cheating on his wife, an observation he doesn't seem to appreciate.

One evening, while driving home from their house, I commented to my wife that I sometimes envied my friend.

"How so?" she asked.

"He never has to wrestle with anything," I said. "Everything is crystal clear. He never doubts. He never questions. He has an answer for everything."

"Why would you envy that?" she asked.

"Because just as soon as I've made up my mind about God and life and what it means to be human, something happens that causes me to rethink it. Just once, I'd like my beliefs to stay the same."

But by the next morning I was in a better mood and had changed my mind. It occurred to me I enjoy the give-and-take, the wrestling, the struggle with ultimate matters. It is hard work, and sometimes I don't know the answers when people come to me seeking clarity and understanding, but I've become a friend to mystery. Mystery has made me a better person. When I was certain of things, I became arrogant and self-righteous, believing I possessed the truth to a degree no one else did. Uncertainty and ambiguity have caused me to be more thoughtful, more careful with my language, less inclined to be dismissive and critical of others' views.* Anyone who knows me knows I'm not always thoughtful, careful, and considerate, but those virtues have become increasingly important to me.

Whenever dogmatism is elevated as a spiritual virtue, doubt will be a sin. But I have learned that humility and curiosity are the pathway to truth. If Galileo hadn't doubted the conventional wisdom of planetary orbits, his groundbreaking work on the solar system would never have happened. In 1633, he was ordered to recant and sentenced to house arrest until his death in 1642. To its credit, the Roman Catholic Church apologized to Galileo in 1992. Unfortunately, he had been dead 350 years, so was unaware of their regret.

The problem with theological certainty is its tendency to harden our hearts, making openness to fresh insights and deeper truths nearly impossible. *So while it's true the seeker is sometimes not quite sure what to believe, it is also true the religiously rigid tend to have difficulty seeing their need for growth.* I know that because I have dwelled in both camps. Now, having unlearned many things I was taught about God, let me conclude this book by telling you about the God who remains.

The Nature and Power of Divine Love

Unlike many Christians, I don't believe Jesus will return again to initiate a new order in which the righteous are rewarded and

---

* Though I admit I have spent a good bit of this book criticizing those views.

the evil are vanquished. Though I have a list of wicked people I would like God to vanquish, I'm not holding my breath. When, and if, justice prevails in the world, it will happen because people of goodwill have made it happen. I see no evidence that God regularly and predictably intervenes in the course of human affairs to set matters right. For much of my life, I believed God did, but my wishing it were so does not increase its likelihood. I realize certain Bible verses suggest such an intervention, but the Bible also suggests that the sun stood still, that people who had been dead for several days were brought back to life, and that the waters of the Nile River were turned into blood. The fact that a handful of biblical texts suggest Jesus will descend from the clouds with an army of angels to set matters right doesn't mean it's likely to happen.

But there is another, more important, reason I don't believe Jesus will return to annihilate evil people. I no longer believe God is vindictive. I no longer believe God uses violence to accomplish her vision for humanity, just as I do not use violence against people to accomplish my goals. I argue, I persuade, I plead, on a few rare occasions I have even insisted someone do as I asked,* but I have never used violence to get my way, or physically harmed another being. I do not believe God's options are so few that he must resort to the wholesale destruction of his children.

Nor do I believe God's prevailing and dominant emotion is wrath. I do not believe God is narcissistic, and therefore angered by those who fail to pay him proper homage. I believe

---

* My two sons. It didn't work.

just the opposite is true, that God is honored by our questions and curiosity, and oddly enough, even honored by our doubts, for they mean we have taken God seriously enough to think deeply about him. Our doubts are evidence that we have engaged God, even if our conclusions about God are not shared by the church.

Wrath is destructive, and therefore utterly opposed to the foremost priority of God, which is to create. It is telling that the first two stories told about God in the Hebrew scriptures are creating stories.* In the first story, God speaks creation into being; in the second story, God forms humans from dust, breathes life into them, then plants a garden and places them there. Each story is beautiful in its own way. What both stories utterly lack is any hint of malevolence. To be sure, that perspective would soon find its way into the Bible, no doubt placed there by malcontents who couldn't imagine responding to human failure with anything but anger.

So God is love, right? Well, that depends on how we understand love. I'm reluctant to ascribe human emotions to God, as if God were an extrapolation of humanity, with all our attendant feelings, emotions, and tendencies magnified to a divine degree. The writer M. Scott Peck defined love as one's commitment to the growth of the beloved. When love is understood that way, we begin to understand the nature of God. *I believe God is that essence in us that reaches out to another, committed*

---

* While these two stories tell about God creating the universe, I don't believe they are historically or scientifically accurate. I do, however, believe these stories are symbolically true, that love creates, not destroys.

to their well-being, their enlightenment, their moral, emotional, relational, and spiritual growth.

Does God have power? Only insofar as love has power. Love can heal division, because love helps us forgive and be reconciled. But if I got pancreatic cancer tomorrow, love couldn't heal that. If I went to a doctor and she told me if I wanted to be healed of cancer I needed to love more fully, I would think she was a kind person and commit myself to loving more deeply, then go in search of another doctor.

Power, like love, takes many forms and has many faces. It isn't enough to say God is powerful, or God is loving; we need to define the scope, focus, and nature of that power and love. Whenever we speak in generalities about God, we almost always make claims that don't withstand careful scrutiny. We overpromise, attributing activities and emotions to God that defy experience and reason. Whatever God is, God is not a supernatural magician, able to suspend reality, able to make fact fiction and fiction fact. No matter what more zealous believers might claim, all things are not possible with God. To believe they are is to set ourselves up for inevitable disappointment and, ironically, unbelief when the things we were taught about God prove unreliable.

We are too often enthralled when speaking of God's power. Too many Christians concede that God isn't universally loving, usually by citing Bible stories about God's destructive, often capricious wrath. But they continue to insist on God's unlimited power, unwilling to admit there are obvious limits to that power. They would rather God be angry and all-powerful than loving and limited in power. I understand this. We live in an arbitrary world, visited by misfortune and injustice we never anticipated and are powerless to resolve. Those who have little access to justice, money, and instruments of power are especially vulnerable. It is a great comfort to believe God has the power and authority we so obviously lack and so desperately need. I think this is why the story of Jesus resonates with the powerless. In him, they see an ally, an advocate, who will stand with them, doing for them what they cannot do for themselves. I understand the appeal of that. I just don't believe it is true, at least to the extent we wish. There are powers and principalities loose in the world, and many good, faithful people suffer mightily at their hands. That is reality. Our assertions about God can't be based on wishful thinking.

But this doesn't mean God is powerless, it means only that God's power isn't exercised in the ways we've customarily believed. From what I can tell, God doesn't appear to be an interventionist, manipulating events to bless and protect us. But there is another power, if I may use that word, which is rooted in God's determination to love. This is the power to stir and expand the human spirit. It is the divine presence and power within each of us that helps us see with new eyes. This Divine Within magnifies truth, helping us first understand ourselves so we can better understand others. It helps us forgive when we are inclined to bear grudges, and strengthens us to persist in the face of evil. I have experienced this power many times in my life and have seen it at work in the lives of others. This presence equips us to rise above our human limitations and love in ways we thought impossible. We have seen this power at work in people like Nelson Mandela, who forgave his jailers. We bore witness to this presence when the Amish parents whose children attending West Nickel Mines School in Lancaster County, Pennsylvania, were slain by Charles Roberts forgave him, then provided comfort and assistance to the wife and daughters he left behind. In our Christian faith, we remember Jesus summoning this presence and forgiving his tormentors from the cross. This Divine Within can overcome the most hardened barrier, the human heart.

God Is with Us

Religion deals in contrasts—heaven and hell, saved and unsaved, grace and wrath, God and Satan, doctrine and heresy, light and dark. These counterparts help us delineate between good and evil, which is useful, but life isn't always tidy, and sometimes more subtlety is needed. This is especially true when we talk about God's nature, since, in the words of John the gospel writer, "no one has ever seen God . . ."* Still, this hasn't kept us from making all sorts of claims about God, and I include myself in that universal "us." Humans excel at God-making.

The church has said God is beyond us and yet within us, both transcendent and immanent. I once heard God described

---

* The full verse reads, "No one has ever seen God; the only Son, who is in the bosom of the Father, he has made him known." I didn't want you to think I was sneaking something past you by quoting John 1:18 only in part. John says Jesus reveals God to us, which makes you think some Christians would take the words of Jesus more seriously than they do, especially the parts about loving our enemies and welcoming the stranger.

as the creative force at the leading edge of the universe's expansion, this cosmic creative power riding the first wave of the Big Bang, fashioning galaxies, throwing off planets and stars and black holes. The imagery is certainly fascinating, and I can see how people might believe that, but I have a hard time wrapping my head around it. I can describe it, I just can't affirm it. Science has proven, at least to my satisfaction, how the universe was formed, how it expands, and how specific lifeforms evolved and took their places in the cosmos.

I can marvel at a tree or flower, be awed by a starlit night, moved by birdsong, but still believe all those things are the products of natural selection, behind which no mastermind, no divine hand carefully and creatively nudging cells into place must be found. When I contemplate creation, my intellect does not demand an affirmation of faith or my assent to a creed. It is enough for me to wonder and appreciate and be grateful for life in all its gorgeous diversity.

What I have never been able to explain, apart from God, is the deep welling up of love when I hold my granddaughter, or witness great compassion. Where is the cell for kindness, the gene for love? Where is the animating force for selfless good? Which muscle gives strength of character? How are we hardwired for dignity? John spoke of a light that dwells in all. This Inward Light is the God I honor. It is the God I have known firsthand. Believing in this God requires no stretch of the imagination, no mental or linguistic gymnastics. This God of Inward Light is as real to me as my own children. It empowers me to be a better person than I sometimes want to be. And not just me but many people I know, people who forgive though they have been dramatically wronged. More times than I can count, I have seen this Light overcome the darkness of retribution. That, to me, is just as much a marvel as any landscape.

I can't imagine a God riding the front waves of creation. Lord knows I've tried. I just can't. If you can, I'm happy for you. Truly. But I now depend upon science to unlock the mysteries of the cosmos. What science has been unable to explain, at least to my satisfaction, is the God Within I have experienced. People like Jesus have revealed this Light, and will continue to do so. You and I can live in the power of this Light and Love. This Light transcends religions, nations, cultures, genders, and eras. It is present in all people everywhere, from Adam and Eve onward.* This Light is the source of all joy, the fountainhead of all love. When we live in its power, we are fully human, living as God intended.

Community, Not Creed, as God's Priority

Though I have moved beyond some of the beliefs taught me by the church, I have held fast to the value of community. I do understand how people can negotiate life without believing in a higher being, having known atheists and agnostics who are perfectly happy. But I have never met a whole and healthy person who lacked loving friendships. For many of us, those friendships occur in spiritual communities. Though I belong to a number of associations and groups, my participation in

---

* No, I don't believe in a literal Adam and Eve. I'm being poetic here. Work with me.

a spiritual community has enabled me to engage the deeper dimensions of life in a way my involvement in secular community hasn't. I'm a member of the ACLU, but the Quaker faith I belong to has been championing issues of justice far longer. My membership in the Sierra Club is meaningful, but religion has advocated for creation care since its earliest days. I support Doctors Without Borders, but religions are responsible for many hospitals around the world. Everything I value has been a historic priority of the world's religions. To divorce myself from spiritual community would be to separate myself from the culture that birthed my life's priorities.

In spiritual community, I have found grace, hope, courage, and direction. I have been exposed to worlds I wouldn't have known, cultures I wouldn't have experienced, and ideas I likely never would have considered. Ironically, even as I have rejected some of the religious precepts of my Quaker community, I have never been ordered or compelled to affirm something I could not in good conscience believe. More times than I can count, I have been urged to follow my leading, even when that leading deviated from historic church practice. For all the criticisms I have heard about the intransigence of the church, and indeed some Christian communities can be headstrong, I have been free to explore, think, and embrace new territory. This book is evidence of that freedom.

This is one of the reasons I return, again and again, to my community in the church. But there are other reasons. Devoting my life to the growth of others has helped me grow. Urging others to listen and forgive has made me listen and forgive. Helping people think and speak more carefully about God and life has caused me to think and speak more carefully. I have been on the verge of leaving several times, when people were unkind or petty, or the demands on my time exhausted me. So I retreated, rested, but then always returned. And have been better for it.

How do we become fully human without one another? How can we learn and grow in isolation? How can we experience happiness, joy, and love apart from others? How can we know God without God's presence being mediated to us through the stories and experiences of others? Growth through community is difficult, even painful, but I know of no other way to grow.

When I was in first grade, my teacher, Mrs. Mann, brought several eggs and an incubator into our classroom. We watched daily, looking for the first crack to appear and a chick to emerge. One day our patience was rewarded when we heard a faint tapping sound and saw a small hole appear in one eggshell. I remember asking Mrs. Mann if we could crack the egg to help the chick be hatched.

"No," she said, "the chick needs to break through the shell to build its strength."

I believe healthy communities function in much the same way. Bumping up against others, negotiating life, breaking through into new realities build our strength. Without this struggle we wither and die. God rarely works solo but works most often in tandem with others, perfecting us, each of us completing one another.

This is the God I believe in, because this is the God I've experienced—this Divine Presence within, committed to our maturation, at work in the arena of the blessed community. I do not know whether God is present at the front of creation. I wasn't there. But I do know God is with us now. I experience her presence every day. I am certain, as certain as one can be about anything, that we have more to learn about God, and more to unlearn. Yet both the learning and the unlearning are great gifts, moving us toward truth, joy, and peace everlasting.

Acknowledgments

_____

I am grateful to the many people who make my life a rich one—my wife, Joan, my sons, Spencer and Sam, my daughters-in-law, Jessica and Kelsea, my granddaughter, Madeline, my fellow Quakers at Fairfield Friends Meeting in Camby, Indiana, and my nonreligious friends who, knowing a man must develop wide interests, sit on my porch and chat about everything but God.

About the Author

Philip Gulley is the pastor of Fairfield Friends Meeting near Indianapolis. He is the author of more than twenty books and hopes to write twenty more. He and his wife, Joan, are the parents of two sons and the grandparents of Madeline.

He also writes monthly columns for the *Saturday Evening Post* and the *Indianapolis Monthly* and has been awarded two Emmys for his work with PBS. A graduate of Marian University and Christian Theological Seminary, he has received two honorary doctorates for his contributions to theology and literature.

In addition to pastoring and writing, Philip enjoys riding his vintage Triumph Bonneville motorcycle, fiddling in his garage, and visiting with his neighbors.